The Man Who Didn't Read or Write

The Man Who Didn't Read or Write

and the woman who said I Do!

Nancy Bennett

ISBN-13: 9780692997734
ISBN-10: 0692997733
Library of Congress Control Number: 2017919234
BennettBooks, Phoenix, AZ

Contents

Preface

ONE DAY AT a coffee shop, an elderly man overheard me describing to some friends the book I had written about my mother. As I was walking away from the group, the gentleman approached me and asked, "Would you be willing to write *my* life story?"

I was enchanted and flattered, but I said, "Sir, I don't know you, I know nothing about you—I don't even know your name! I could help you, but why don't you write it yourself?"

He responded immediately, "Why, because I can't read *or* write!"

I was hooked.

He wasn't finished. "But I retired with a million dollars after forty years with the same company!"

My background as a special-education teacher gives me the knowledge to be amazed at his success in spite of his profound illiteracy. US statistics indicate that 70 percent of the adult American prison population is composed of people who either cannot read or read poorly—illiteracy condemns so many to unfulfilled lives. Even though writing was not my first (or only) career, of course I would write his story, because I knew it was important the moment he told me about himself. He is an inspiration to me, and I expect he will be one to others as well. Another amazing aspect of his story is the large number of people who have gone through George's life without knowing he was illiterate. I was especially surprised at one of the retirement activities he pursues, and I think you will be too.

Along the way, George encountered another handicapping condition, but that, too, he has managed, one day at a time.

I hope I have done justice to George and his delightful wife, Spunky. They are tops in my book.

Acknowledgements

GEORGE AND SPUNKY deserve so much thanks and praise for their work with me on this book—and thanks, George, for asking me to write it. The experience has been a blessing.

A few of George's friends gave me input on his life—but let's face it, he's 83...some of them are no longer around! That's why these fellows were so important, as was the input from George and Spunky. Thanks to Don Hall, Larry Hempan, and Dr. Charles Vawter. A great help were the records departments of the following school districts: Creighton Elementary School District, Phoenix Union High School District, and Phoenix College Community College District. (Thanks for keeping records forever!)

Mary Peralta of *Inside Willo* deserves thanks for her article about the Ernsts many years ago, which gave me the big picture of the Ernsts life together.

Thanks so much to my Beta-Readers Lynn Engle, Diane Horn, Fred Bennett, Wally Book, Sarah Privee, and Jack Wick. You gave me helpful and honest input.

Lastly, only because it is the last thing I did before production—I want to thank my Title Survey participants for their quick and fun assistance with help determining the title of this book, several of you whom I met only in passing for this project: Jack W., Fred B., Diane H., Frank S., Theresa and Mike C., Jim. R., Lisa H., Nancy C., Patch and his mother, Bruce J., Terrence S., Karen T., Erick M., Cynthia K., Rene & Angel D., Wally B., Lauren, Melinda, Betty H., Glenna, Patti, Alex, Gene, Stu., Mike, Lori, and Mark.

Of course I could not have seen this book come to fruition if not for the knowledgeable, competent and patient staff at CreateSpace. Thank you so much.

Part 1

CHAPTER 1

─────── ✂ ───────

In the Navy

"GEORGE, HOW ARE we gonna get in the navy? You can't read, and I'm flat footed!"

Bill Cramer was serious. He had seen George get by with some amazing stuff throughout their friendship, but this looked impossible. This was the US Navy, and people didn't just fool the navy!

"Bill, first of all, my not reading is the easy part. You're gonna fill out my forms to get me in. And about your flat feet—I have a plan. Let me show you."

They practiced George's plan the rest of the afternoon and agreed. "Let's go for it. Nothing to lose," they both said. At the recruiter's office the next day, they picked up the paperwork and took it home. Bill filled out his and George's paperwork. When they were called in for their group medicals, they were ready. Another friend had described the process to them, so they knew the doc would be looking at two body parts—both below the belt. The part they had to concentrate on was the feet.

The friends stood in a line two deep of shower-bare recruits of all sizes and colors, all facing forward. The doc came along on a rolling chair, asking each to pick up his right foot and then his left foot. Bill stood in the line behind George. Doc looked at George's right and then his left foot and checked off "No" in the flatfoot box. With a bit of planned distraction, George surreptitiously stepped back and traded places with Bill, who took his place in the line that had already been checked. In that way, the doc checked George's feet again and Bill's not at all...pass!

Joining the US Navy in October of 1953, historically speaking, would seem to be a safe period to do military service. The Korean War had ended in July, and President Dwight D. Eisenhower, a man with a distaste for war born of his experience and determination to keep us out of the emerging Cold War through strength of weaponry and diplomacy, had been swept into office the previous November by a landslide. George would have the honor of serving under the greatest Commander in Chief America had known since George Washington. Under a different man's leadership, George's military service could have been dangerous, but it wasn't. There were still recruitment quotas to be met, so upon getting cleared for duty medically and otherwise, these two imperfect young men heard the words they wanted to hear:

"Welcome aboard, men. You're in the navy now!"

CHAPTER 2

— ✂ —

Back to the Beginning

HE MAY NOT have been the greatest-looking kid born in the city of Wilkes-Barre, Pennsylvania, on June 23, 1934, but his father didn't care; dads don't usually have the same starry-eyed impression of their newborn babies that their mothers do. George Ernst had been told to expect a wrinkled, red, scrawny little tad, and that's what he got. Still, George Ernst—now Sr.—thought the kid looked like a winner. As for himself, he knew he was now a changed man, a man with the responsibility to bring this boy, George Jr., through the formative years of his life, and he relished the thought.

"I'm a dad, Karl, and I've got a boy!"

"Sure. I noticed that, since I delivered him, George. He's fine, as far as I can see, and Mom's doing fine, as well. Go see her." Dr. Karl Ernst had been the chosen delivery doc for sentimental reasons. He was George Sr.'s brother.

The proud new father went to his wife's side and held her hand. "Marian, we've got us a great little boy, George Jr."

And Mom smiled weakly and asked to see her baby.

While Marian had been laboring to produce an heir to the twenty-one-year-old George, the world at large outside the hospital doors carried on as it had planned. President Franklin D. Roosevelt was spending a two-day holiday at the family home in Hyde Park, New York. He had plans to eradicate the financial depression that had taken hold in the United States and elsewhere since the stock market crash of 1929. Here and elsewhere, most politicians and world leaders labored to keep the peace of the post–Great War era, while Nazis in Europe were actually taking steps that would lead to the next one.

On the day of George Jr.'s birth, the front page of the *Evening News* of Luzerne County reported that minor officials in Germany had mutinied and been taken to concentration camps, and the chancellor of Austria had been removed and reassigned. Whether we knew it or not, and most ordinary Americans did not, Adolf Hitler had just made a move on Austria, which later became the land of *The Sound of Music*. Luzerne County had a large population of people whose grandparents had emigrated from Germany in the late 1800s, including the fathers of Francis and Mary Ernst, George Sr.'s parents. The elder Ernsts would pay attention to the world tomorrow. But Marian and the baby were healthy, and the Reverend William Healey had performed the baptism minutes after George Jr.'s birth; thus, the infant Ernst became a full-fledged Irish American Catholic boy on day one. For now, the rest of the world would fade from view while the proud family celebrated the birth of its newest member!

CHAPTER 3

—— ✽ ——

A Delightful Childhood

GEORGE JR. WAS born into an enviable extended family among members who got along and cared about each other.

"I had a dream childhood," George recalled. "There was a lot of love."

His young parents, both only twenty-one at his birth, both attractive and fit, doted on him and kept him a single child until ten years later. That didn't mean he was a lonely child; he had the benefit of the extended family that so many who have such an arrangement reflect on with pride and that others of us imagine longingly. George and his parents lived on the top floor of a three-story house, known in Wilkes-Barre as a "Father, Son, and Holy Ghost" home. The second floor housed George Sr.'s parents. The two—now three—generations shared the dining room, kitchen, and parlor on the ground floor. Little George, now called Georgie to distinguish him from his father, was close to both grandparents, and they also lavished attention on him and adored him. He had built-in neighborhood playmates, most of them cousins. His aunt Kutsy's son Michael was somewhat younger than Georgie, and they played together a lot, but several of the kids were older. The cousins didn't care.

Even as a preschooler, Georgie had free range over the blocks surrounding his house at 39 Stanley Street, where cousins, aunts, and uncles populated the neighborhood. The personable little scamp made himself welcome everywhere, including at the local business establishments. "When I was a little kid, our family would go to the Italian restaurant every Friday night. I'd go right into the kitchen to say hi to the guys in the kitchen. They all knew me—'Hi, Georgie!' they'd all say. I knew everybody!" said George.

Grandpa Ernst was a fine gentleman whose father had been born in Bavaria and his sainted mother in Ireland, together providing the boy with his German last name and his Irish sense of whimsy. He owned a cigar factory and storefront in town within a short walking distance from the Father, Son, and Holy Ghost home. At four or five years of age, his grandson Georgie was a constant visitor to the shop. During the latter part of the afternoon, he would walk to the store and join the men congregating there to smoke and discuss world and local events. George would get a pretzel and a soda and sit down and soak up the conversation. When saturated with contemporary talk among the customers, he would go into the back room where the cigars were made. While the German workers rolled the cigars, other men would read aloud to them in English from books, magazines, and newspapers. He loved to sit and listen while they read.

"Georgie, when you get older, you can be a reader for the workers," Grandpa promised.

At closing time, Georgie would lock the back and front doors for Grandpa. As they walked home together, hand in hand, about halfway there, Grandpa would stop and ask, "Georgie, did we lock that door?"

And always he would reply, "Yes, Grandpa, we did."

Grandpa would then say, "Well, it's better to be safe. Let's just go back and check." They would go back, and sure enough, the door was always locked. Young but conscientious Georgie already knew the meaning of responsibility at that age, and his memory was as sharp as any child's would be. He didn't mind going back and forth; it was more time with Grandpa.

The Ernst home was in very close proximity to the Susquehanna River, a river that flooded with regularity. When it did, young Georgie and his cousins entertained themselves by throwing a ball out the back door and running through the house to catch it as the river flowed by the front door. That's a frighteningly close body of fast-moving water! From this great river, he acquired a pet duck that followed him around, which he named Nathan. He's not sure why or how he chose that name, but that's the name he chose. He must have had his reasons.

When he wasn't throwing a ball into the flooding river, he would sit close enough to the nearby railroad tracks to count the cars as they went by, thereby teaching himself—with the help of his older friends—how to count.

He recalls picking peaches by the bushelful from their trees in the backyard and being sent to the cellar to retrieve them when his mother needed some for a meal. One day when he had his cousin Michael in tow, his mother said, "Go down to the cellar, Georgie, and get some peaches for my pie. And don't take all day!"

He and Michael looked at each other and took off with great haste down into the cellar, skipping steps, bumping each other, and racing to the bottom. That basement with the Lionel train set his dad had assembled there was quite the draw for Georgie and his friends. And there was another draw the boys had found in the basement.

"C'mon, Michael. Get in the coal bin. We'll have a go at it," said George.

That particular day, forgetting the peaches, they scrambled into the coal bin, where they conducted a wrestling match. There were two separate bins that held different types of coal: the large-chunk bin, which fed the downstairs fire, and the small-chunk bin, which fed the kitchen fire. On this coal-wrestling occasion, somehow a piece of the small-chunk coal breached George's corduroy knickers and impaled his knee. So off he went to Uncle Karl's medical office for an extraction and stitches.

"That coal bin was a big thing," said Georgie.

Boys have always loved to get dirty! Of course, his mother and grandmother had to deal with the black dust on his clothes and hands and face after each bout of coal rassling.

As a child, George had a predilection for placing himself in danger, as the following examples will show.

Dog Bite!

"Down the street from our house was a cherry tree in a neighbor's backyard. They kept a chow dog attached to the clothesline. My cousin would tease and otherwise distract the dog at the far end of the clothesline, and I would climb the tree and get a bunch of cherries and put them down my shirt. One time I slipped coming down and fell out of the tree. That dog turned and tore down to me as I lay dazed on the ground. He attacked me. He nearly tore the cheek off my butt—somehow I was able to get up and run home, with my cousin fast behind me. When I fell, the cherries got squished in my shirt. I ran in the house and yelled to my grandma; she thought my stomach had exploded. She tore open my shirt and started screaming...I yelled, "No, Grandma, it's my hiney! My hiney!" She took me to my uncle's office, and I got stitches in my butt."

Baseball Injury

This particular injury may have been his worst. Sometime before school age, George was playing a game of pickup baseball with his cousins and friends. Many of them were older, but no one ever said that George and his younger cousins couldn't play with them; still, they didn't make it a "baby game," because that's not how boys played then. They played ball with whatever ball was on the scene, which usually was a hardball. If someone got hit with a bat or a ball, well, that just happened. Blood was easy to stanch, and bumps were not that unusual.

George was up to bat, and as he leaned into the pitch, the ball went high for a kid his size and bonked him on the left side of his forehead hard enough to break the skin. He had to sit down. The ball was hard. He was a little dazed, and his vision blurred for a while. He already had a lazy eye that looked slightly inward, not straight ahead. Someone teased him: "Maybe that cross-eye will straighten up, Georgie."

He likely started to bleed from the gash, and he might have dabbed it with his shirt. Maybe Mom or Grandma applied a bit of mercurochrome when he got home. His mother must have taken him over to Uncle Karl's office for some stitches, because the evidence is right there at the top of his forehead.

"I was becoming a human pincushion. Stitches here, stitches there—I thought nothing of it," said George.

CHAPTER 4

Childhood with Mom and Dad

THE GREAT DEPRESSION of the 1930s created work shortages for men of the Wilkes-Barre factories, as it did elsewhere, and the coal mines of the great coal state of Pennsylvania had declined due to an increase in oil, gas, and electricity usage. None of that impacted George Sr. He had fallen into the one job never to go out of style: the sale and marketing of distilled whiskey. His original position and the one George recalls most fondly was that of the fellow who hung the crepe advertising window displays for the Schenley Whiskey Company, which had seamlessly transitioned from a manufacturer of "medicinal" whiskey to a nationwide distributer of fine bourbon immediately after the repeal of Prohibition in December of 1933. Schenley was one of the largest whiskey producers in the country, with a distillery nearby in Schenley, Pennsylvania.

So while little George sat around in his grandpa's cigar store, soaking up man talk, George Sr. traipsed around town to all the bars, where fellows were sitting around having the same conversations. Work—when would the coal mines outside town reopen; the Depression—how'd that damn Herbert Hoover manage to let it get so bad; politics—Franklin Roosevelt sounds like he has the answers, so it's time for the government to help us, not hurt us; and sports—by 1936, the New York Yankees had started on a four-year run of championships; too bad the Pirates couldn't make it to the World Series like they did in 1909, when they had won with Honus Wagner.

"Dad, can I go with you to watch you hang the crepe in the windows today?" Georgie would implore.

"No, son, there's nothing for you to do in a stinky old bar. Your mom can bring you by on Saturday, and you can look at it then." Didn't Dad know how much Georgie loved the stinky old cigar shop?

Along with his work as a display artist, George Sr. supplied the bartenders and liquor-store proprietors with the little two-ounce samples of whiskey to hand out as incentives. George Sr. proved to be a role model of ingenuity for his son, at least at saving money and space. Instead of an box spring under his son's mattress, he stored his boxes of little whiskey samples there, right under his son's precious little head. And torso. And legs and arms. The irony of this arrangement would be realized later in his life. For now, it was just part of his bed.

"Help me put your mattress back up, Georgie. That's it—OK, go to bed now."

One job wasn't enough for George Sr. Perhaps he was paid on commission, which is inconsistent; perhaps he was ambitious; or perhaps he just liked to work. So he took a part-time weekend gig. The best-known company in town was the Planters Peanut Company, started right there in Wilkes-Barre in 1906 by two enterprising Italian immigrants whose talents were suited to the American entrepreneurial spirit. Frequently on the weekends to earn extra money, George Sr. would don the costume of Planter's Mr. Peanut—that tall, dapper national icon—and saunter about town in a top hat and leggings under a gigantic plastic peanut shell, passing out samples and bringing goodwill to the town. When George and his mom were out and about on Saturdays, they would always see the peanut, and if she knew it was her husband, she would say, "Look, Georgie, there's your dad. He's Mr. Peanut today."

What better job could a father have?

And of course, there were the childhood traditions his parents and the city of Wilkes-Barre perpetuated. George said, "I was five or six and still thought there was a Santa Claus. On Christmas Eve, there was no tree up or anything. My family left the glass of milk and cookies. In the morning, the tree was up, the gifts were there, and the milk was half drunk.

"There was a fellow who would fly his plane under the bridge over the river on the Fourth of July every year. It was a biplane. He did tricks and turns, and flew low over the crowd. That was the big thing every year. Afterward, the fireworks.

"And the circus! In June, my friends and I would go to the Barnum and Bailey Circus. We'd go early and water the elephants to get in free. We did that every summer, probably from age six to twelve. We were regulars at the circus!"

CHAPTER 5

First Grade!

AH, SCHOOL. HOW would that go for the little guy, a boy happy to spend hours playing outside with cousins, accompanying Grandpa from work, and entertaining himself, now that that potentially wonder-filled, life-changing event was upon him? The time to go to school would occur, but would he like it? Was he excited about going? Absolutely yes. He knew that when he learned to read, he would be able to read to the workers in Grandpa's cigar factory.

First grade. George stood straight and still in his blue knickers and white button-down shirt, waiting for Sister Mary Agnes to open the classroom door and allow her new students to march in and find their seats. He was still that scrawny, wiry kid his dad had seen the day he was born, not the tallest in the line but not the smallest, wearing his first pair of eyeglasses his uncle, Dr. Frank, had prescribed and fitted the week before school. His right eye looked inward; the glasses were expected to help with that. He already could count—that had come naturally by watching the railroad cars chug through town. But reading! Now he would be able to learn to unlock the mystery of those letters his mom had shown him and tried to teach him while reading to him from his bedtime stories. Would his lazy eye bother him? He fidgeted a bit, thinking of that. Would the kids he didn't already know tease him about it?

After hearing the sister's instructions about waiting in line and entering the classroom quietly, he marched in with the others, tall and somber. So this was the classroom. He could hear his footsteps causing the shiny wooden floors to creak; he could smell the mixture of wax and chalk in the air. The walls were so close—he realized he would be in a closed environment for hours every day, taking up time he could be playing outside and "working" with Grandpa, except for lunch and recess. So he'd better make the best of it. He'd be sure to obey Sister Mary Agnes. He would apply himself— a term his father had used several times while preparing him for the rigors of school. It would be his job, his dad had told him, which he welcomed, even as a child, because he had seen his father work so hard, and he had even been part of Grandpa's work at the cigar store. Now he would have his own work—the ABCs!

Bad News at School

And then came the first parent-teacher conference.

"Mrs. Ernst, we have a few concerns about George. No, no, he's a perfectly good boy, very respectful, kind, has a good time with friends. But we are concerned with his right eye. Has Dr. Ernst ever voiced any concern for that eye? As an ophthalmologist, does he have any ideas about it? Because George is having a hard time learning the letters, which is the most important task of a child in first grade. He says he has trouble seeing the board. Oh, he's fine with the numbers—at least, he can count out loud—but it's the letters he isn't learning. He's falling behind."

That did it. Marian always found it ironic that both her brothers-in-law were doctors—one the man who had delivered Georgie, and the other an ophthalmologist—but neither had thought of treating Georgie's lazy eye with anything other than prescription glasses, which wasn't working. She had been concerned enough about it herself for several years. Her ophthalmologist brother-in-law had said, "It will straighten out." Now she had some ammunition—the concern of the sister.

"George, tell your brother that Georgie's eye is keeping him from learning his letters. What can we do? He said it would straighten out by the time he went to school. It hasn't. He's seven years old," Georgie's mom told Dad.

And by the end of the week, Dr. Frank Ernst had arranged for the doctors at Mayo Clinic in Rochester, Minnesota, to see George. The family would go during summer break, right after George came home with the "great" news that he had *not* been promoted to second grade.

"I ran all the way home. My grandma was standing in the kitchen at the sink, and I showed her the report card. 'Look, Grandma! The sister likes me so much she wants me to be in her class again next year!' My grandma chuckled and said, 'No, Georgie, it's because you didn't learn how to read!'" George recounted.

CHAPTER 6

— ❧ —

Sleeping in the Car at Mayo

GEORGE REMEMBERED, "WE drove up to that building in Rochester, and I was scared. Would they have to cut into my eye? How could they fix it? What secret treatment would they come up with to fix this right eye? And I did want it fixed. Trying to focus the eye was tiring, especially now in school. Even though most of the kids were used to it and didn't tease me, it seemed to make my schoolwork harder to do."

The trip to Mayo had been an adventure in itself. To stay for a string of appointments, they would need to spend at least a week there. That was a problem. Hotel rooms cost money, and although the Ernsts had income, George's dad had a very strict attitude about spending money. OK, he was cheap. In his defense, he hadn't thought they would be staying more than one day. OK, he was also unrealistic. How had he thought his little boy's cross-eye, which had been that way for quite a while, would just go away upon seeing a specialist for the first time? He knew there would likely be no surgery—Marian had been vehemently opposed to that.

So they slept in the car for a week. A nice, large sedan, with bench seats in front and back? Not exactly. Look up the '42 Ford, with the two seats in the back that went down. It must have been very uncomfortable. But there they stayed. And it was cold at night, not winter cold, but summer-night cold, as it gets in Minnesota.

The mysterious treatment the eye doctors devised at Mayo was a patch. A simple patch over his left eye to force the right eye to straighten up. In fact, it was so simple, it didn't work at first. The patch didn't have a chance against George, the kid who could think of all sorts of entertainment for himself and could, as we will see, always find a solution or a way around an impediment. Because the patch fit over his left eyeglass lens, it didn't cover his peripheral vision. In his first public act of beating the system, the creative little cheater simply turned his head to look out the side of his glasses. Not for long though. Knowing they had been beat, the docs taught Georgie some exercises to use with his right eye while wearing the patch, and not too long afterward, with the insistence of his parents that he do the exercises, that eye had straightened out. Now would he learn his ABCs?

CHAPTER 7

Foreboding

RETAINING GEORGE IN the first grade and giving him the lazy-eye treatment didn't bring the reading cure George and his family had hoped for and rather expected. As he continued in grade one for the second time, he learned the letters for a day or two and then—poof! They were gone. The sister and her superiors in the school were baffled. One older sister had a recollection of a student like George—a boy who hadn't been able to keep the letters in his head for more than the day he learned them. She had spent much time trying to help him, including tutoring him after school. She had to report that it never stuck.

"Sister, what happened to that boy?" the other sisters wondered.

"He left school in the fifth grade. He's a grown man now and still in town, working in a mine. That's where these boys usually end up. There or in prison. Prisons are full of people who didn't learn to read for one reason or another."

The room went silent. That wouldn't do for George Ernst.

"Why do you think that boy didn't learn to read, Sister?"

"Because he couldn't. It's not a case of will or discipline or 'stick-to-it-iveness' or trying harder. It's a matter of brain development or perhaps even injury. And your George sounds just like him. What do we know about him, other than this deficiency and that he's a sweet little boy who likes to help the teacher? Think of another way to help him feel self-confident, because it won't be by learning to read."

This was startling news to Sister Mary Agnes. She had so hoped that George's eye had been the problem. She certainly didn't want her student to end up in prison. She had noticed that during his first year in school, he had become increasingly nervous and seemed to be compensating for his disability by talking a mile a minute. The sisters had started telling him he had to slow down or he would become tongue tied.

"What shall we do about his nervous talk, Sister?"

The experienced sister replied, "I have found that a mouthful of pretzels helps. Give him a pretzel, and ask him to chew it and talk at the same time. It works after a few weeks. Keep it up. And about the confidence factor, sit him in the front row by the door. When I visit the classroom or when the priests drop in, and especially if the monsignor is touring the classrooms, assign Georgie to be the escort. He is to answer the door and walk the visitor to your desk and introduce him or her to you. It's an important responsibility. And don't forget to use picture stories to teach your lessons. Paint a picture with words when you tell stories about people and places. Draw on the board! And let all the children—not just George—draw pictures of stories or history lessons that you teach. Engage him and keep trying. Something might click. Something might work. Try to teach him words—I know, I know, the "whole language" method is not approved here, but just in case, try teaching him some whole words."

George never experienced punishment at his Catholic school for not reading. He doesn't remember anyone pulling him aside and talking to him about his reading. It's clear that rumors of mean, punishing nuns didn't apply where George was concerned. He was a loving, outgoing child who needed support, and his teachers provided it.

So that is how George spent his second year in grade one. It wasn't bad, and he perceived his role as classroom greeter to be the result of being the teacher's pet. The sister didn't do anything to contradict that thinking on his part, which made her pretzel cure tolerable to George, and he didn't fight it. Besides that, the sister and his parents warned him that he would become tongue tied if he didn't slow down—whatever that meant! It didn't mean that his tongue was "tied down," but the threat coupled with the pretzels was a good way to get him to slow down.

CHAPTER 8

—— ⌘ ——

Life at Home with a Nonreader

IT HAS NEVER been easy for parents of learning-disabled children to get on board with the concept of disability. The first response is usually "Not my kid!" Then, "Is he trying? Is he applying himself?" Then, "What is the teacher doing wrong? Why can't the school teach him?" Then comes "Is he slow? Retarded?" and finally, "What can we do?" It's similar to the grieving process, including the bargaining, like "What if we got him yet another teacher?" There's depression and reflection—"Why us? What have we done wrong?"—and finally, the acceptance and hope. "He has other wonderful qualities. He'll learn to read someday." George's parents had their golden boy, and day after day, year after year, they loved him just the same. He has only good memories of his childhood and his parents, as can be seen in his recollection below.

"My mom was my soul mate. Very happy; she liked everything she did. She'd do the wash, and then, when ready to hang it on the line, she'd throw all the pins on the ground first. I asked her why she did that, and she said, 'That's how I get my exercise, Georgie!'

"She was beautiful, like a movie star. Blue eyes, small features. I never saw another mom so pretty as mine. And she stayed that way her whole life.

"My dad was a good dad. I only kissed him twice in my life, once when he was sick enough to have the priest called in. He was a hard worker. Sure, he played with me a bit, but basically, he was a hard worker. I loved my dad.

"I had a dream life—there were never any shootings, accidents, or family arguments. I never heard my mother complain that Dad wasn't making enough money, or anything like that. They didn't fight.

"I didn't have depression about not reading. I just kept listening in class and of course getting my little girlfriend to help me with my homework, by giving me her paper to copy. Yeah, I cheated some. You know, spelling words, things like that. But I just kept trying, and I guess I didn't know how poor my writing was. I just didn't know.

"I had fun at school and after school. On icy days, my pals and I would hang on the fender of the school bus and let it drag us. I was one of the best. I would be first to run to the side without the exhaust, and my best friend would hang onto me around my waist. He'd yell, 'Hang on, George! Hang on!'

"All my childhood activities were fun, except for going to the graveyard after Mass! No matter how I'd try to get out of going to the graveyard—I'd tell Mom, 'I have to go to the bathroom!' --she always made me go along. She usually had to bribe me with ice cream afterward at the drugstore. And I *did* have to go to the bathroom—my cousins and I always peed on Uncle Winfield's grave. Not because we didn't like him, but his big headstone obscured us from the family."

CHAPTER 9

—— ❧ ——

A Life Mate Is Born

ONE FRIGID FEBRUARY day in 1939, about the time of day when four-and-a-half-year-old George would have been walking his grandpa home from the cigar shop, twenty-three-year-old Anita Diaz Jaurequi was delivering an infant girl to her husband Roberto, and by extension, to the whole town of Jerome, Arizona, over one thousand miles away from Wilkes-Barre.

Jerome was a small mining town clinging to the side of Cleopatra Hill in the northern part of the state, at about five thousand feet above sea level. It would have been about thirty-two degrees that day, cold enough for Señor Jaurequi to wish he didn't have to go down into the mine for two reasons: one, the miserable cold, and the other, the birth of his third daughter, the first by Anita.

Roberto Jaurequi had traveled from Nochistan, Mexico, to work in the Phelps Dodge copper mine, one of several that had made Jerome a town and not merely houses on the side of a hill. Anita was the daughter of Basque parentage, and her father had also come there to work in an earlier mine.

The auspicious day of the birth was Groundhog Day. Grandpa Ernst might have been explaining to George that local and bewildering custom, which had started nearby in Punxsutawney, Pennsylvania. It's likely that the miners in Jerome were not discussing that, and they wouldn't have even read a paper that day, because no local paper was published in Jerome on a regular basis that year. The *Arizona Republic* did make its way over the escarpment from the Valley of the Sun—Phoenix—so they would have eventually read the headlines of the day. On the day little Mary Helen was born, the headline of the *Republic* warned, "Winter's Icy Fingers Clutch at Arizona." In 1939, before it became a mecca for lovers of warmth, American citizens in the rest of the country probably would have been surprised to hear that Arizona had freezing weather in some parts of the state. The town of Jerome and other mountainous areas could get especially cold.

Before statehood in 1912, Jerome had become the fourth-largest town in Arizona, due to the prolific ore mines located in the valley below it. Precious metals had been vital to the modernization of the United States for decades. One mine, the Little Daisy Mine, had become phenomenally profitable, producing in one year alone $10 million of copper, silver, and gold. The mines were fewer now, and they would eventually be depleted, but for now, men like Señor Diaz and Señor Jaurequi would keep coming in and out of the country to work them.

Although not officially a company town, Jerome existed mainly for the support of the mines; its residents were interested in little else, and they did little else than work the mine or feed the miners and educate their children. But by the '30s, the population had decreased from the heyday of the '20s, when 4,000 people lived in Jerome, to now one half that, about 2,200 residents. On a positive note, enough "decent" women had moved in as wives and displaced the preterritorial "working girls" that the town had established a degree of respectability not evident in the late 1800s or early 1900s. Now, families and single miners of several different nationalities lived there together and shared communal small-town lives. Mining records from 1930 suggest that at least 60 percent of the families in town were Latino. Into this welcoming milieu popped little Mary Helen Jaurequi, and it is doubtful the town would ever be the same.

Jerome was definitely not a traditional company town, those of dull architecture and identified by box houses painted a flat gray;

rather, it evoked primarily late-1800s neoclassical or Spanish Revival interpretations. Along the main street, the founders had built typical small-town storefronts leaning against each other, giving the illusion that they were holding each other up against the possibility of sliding down the hill. Overlooking the town from the top of the hill was the out of scale, large, white brick hospital where Mary Helen had been delivered by Dr. Robert Hilton. Around the bend in the road on Clark Street, the two-story red brick grammar-school building was as grand and imposing as those in any American town, and full of the same laughing, learning students. Most of them happened to be of Mexican descent, but they were learning English, of course. And important to the Jaurequi and other Latino families in town was the Spanish Revival–styled Holy Family Catholic Church, compactly built on a slanted section of Highway 89 with a view of the Verde Valley below and the open pit mine.

While "winter's icy fingers clutched at Arizona," the European war was clutching at the politicians in Washington, DC, enticing the president—still FDR—to join in. Americans in the hinterlands and their representatives in the seat of government were still resisting and trying to stay out of it. Nearly five years had elapsed since Hitler had made his move on Austria the day George was born. While the United States had been able to stay somewhat aloof of the occurrences in Europe, it did provide some financial aid and weaponry to France and Great Britain. On the day Mary Helen was born the two-inch *Arizona Republic* headline read, "Aid to France Denounced," and headlines on separate articles read, "Senators Seek Facts on Sale of War Planes" and "War Peril Voiced by Hoover."

But the most chilling header of all was "Hitler Stand Has Merits."

Yes, we had apologists for the mad führer in America before our involvement. A major shift in world events had occurred between George's birth and Mary Helen's—the earlier headlines were about "them." Now they were about "us."

CHAPTER 10

ళ

Childhoods

ACROSS THE COUNTRY in Wilkes-Barre, little George may have heard some talk about the war and the German dictator Hitler while he spent many childhood hours hanging around the cigar store or sitting still with his pretzel and soda listening to the readers in the back room. Grandpa would have shielded him from worry but not from reality—men talked openly in male bastions. Being so young, he wouldn't have understood the details, but he may have heard the talk.

A year and a half later, when he entered first grade, Mary Helen was a toddling one-and-a-half-year-old, meeting all the targets for toddling, walking, speaking, and adorability. Their childhoods, although miles away from each other, were so similar it just seems eerie. Both had happy families, each with strong ties to their cultural heritages. Both families were intact with extended members nearby. Both sets of parents adored and doted on their children, and both were either reaping the benefits of the American dream or getting closer to it each day—Grandpa Ernst owned his own shop, and the Jaurequi family was opening a restaurant in the hotel they had acquired next door to their home on Clark Street.

The food of their cultures was important to both families. The Ernst women made creamy scalloped Irish potatoes with ham, lemon meringue pie, and warm shredded wheat for breakfast. Another breakfast staple was eggnog—without the booze, of course. George remembers the smell of limburger cheese on Friday nights when the family would have other couples in to play cards and socialize. Because the limburger smelled so bad to George, Marian, always thinking of others, would roll up towels and put them under the doors around the house to keep the rank odor out of George's room. George cannot stand limburger cheese to this day.

Mary Helen's mother, Spanish by birth and Mexican by marriage, made cooking her priority and learned many of her mother-in-law's Mexican recipes before opening her own restaurant. She didn't cook the foods of her Basque ancestry; instead, she focused on what Arizonans loved and craved—simple foods such as green chili burritos and red enchiladas.

And then there was their religion. Both families practiced mid-twentieth-century American Catholicism, which was conservative, devout, and very religious. Both families did Mass on Sunday, and the Latin Mass was said. Mary Helen wore a fluffy white dress to her first Communion, just like all little Catholic girls did, and George dressed in a little wool suit with knickers, a white shirt, and a bow tie for his. On regular Sundays, they dressed in conservative and appropriate clothing. That meant little dresses for little girls and shiny church shoes for both.

So on two ends of the country, nearly opposite both north to south and east to west, grew two distinctly delightful American children, much alike. One cultural difference existed in the way these two families celebrated a Catholic death—the Irish Ernsts of Wilkes-Barre held wakes in their home, the bodies of their relatives lying in state in the parlor. "Aw, Mom! Do we have to go to Uncle Joe's wake? Mom, the bodies stink!" George said. The Jaurequis used the more modern method of mourning their dearly departed loved ones in the mortuary.

Childhood in Jerome circa the 1940s was just as fraught with danger as childhood in Wilkes-Barre. Where one had a raging river that flooded regularly, the other had steep hills right out the front and back doors of their homes. Not many little kids rode bicycles in Jerome. Rollovers and crashes on bikes would have kept the place looking like a roller derby or bumper-car grid. A miskicked ball could go either into the river or down a rocky hill, depending on which town you were in. Still, there was plenty to do in each town, and children had the opportunity to discover fun and entertainment in those days that would drive a helicopter parent to an anxiety attack.

Mary Helen was well behaved with her papa, not because it was her basic nature but because it was her father's nature to spank her with a belt if she talked back, if she disobeyed, or if she showed any bit of rebellion to him. Her papa's parents had not kept close tabs on him, and he knew he himself was undisciplined. Roberto wouldn't make that mistake with his girls, including the two daughters he had brought to his marriage with Anita. Yet by the time she was nearly three, the littlest Jaurequi was developing into quite a force, even while being obedient to Papa. With Mama, she could stamp her feet, stand her ground, and scream, "No!" Mama seemed somewhat blasé about her vivacious, personality-plus daughter. At the age of two going on three, Mary Helen had received from her mother the nickname that would describe her perfectly and be used by all who knew her for the rest of her life—Spunky.

᠅

CHAPTER 11

We Go to War, and George Does Battle at School

ON DECEMBER 7, 1941, George was seven and a half years old and happily into his second try at first grade. Mary Helen—now Spunky--was nearly three years old and was already displaying a vivacious personality with a good dose of individualism and stubbornness. The event that brought the United States into World War II occurred far away from either of their homes, but surely their parents were talking about it. The day after Pearl Harbor was bombed, President Roosevelt declared war against Japan, which, because Japan and Germany were allies, brought us into the war against Germany. The talk in Wilkes-Barre must surely have escalated. What great fortune for both George and Spunky to be born so close to WWII, to be too young to go or lose a sweetheart there. They would experience no loss of a father in it—neither was called to go. This was a good time to be a child. Very little about the war fazed either child at all. They went on with their innocent little lives, George trying to learn to read and write and Spunky learning to navigate her way as a feisty toddler.

D-Day

The tide of the war had turned with the literal tide on June 6, 1944, on the beaches of Normandy, France. The man who nine years later would become the president of the United States oversaw and implemented the greatest invasion ever known at that time and since. General Dwight D. Eisenhower directed 4,000 invasion ships, 600 warships, 10,000 planes, and 176,000 Allied servicemen toward and onto those beaches and showed the world the mighty military power of the Western world.

On D-day, Spunky would have been five years and five months old and ready for school. The red brick schoolhouse was just around the sharp bend in the road down the street from her family home, and she could walk to school with her sisters. She loved her teacher, Miss Mice—a great name for a kindergarten teacher. Kindergarten was only three hours long in those days, so there was plenty of time for a nap and playtime when she got home. At home, she would play alone in the house and wait for her dad to get home from the mine or go outside with her friends. Her sisters had a longer school day, and her mom was always busy, taking care of the single boarders the Jaurequis had opened their home to and which the mines always provided.

George was eighteen days short of being ten years old on D-day. On June 22, 1944, the day before his birthday, the GI Bill of Rights law was passed, which included a promised GI home loan for people who served in the military, which he would one day. For now, D-day for him was just part of his summer break, a welcome relief.

At this young age, he was fighting his own personal battle during the school year, and it had certainly not gotten any easier, even though he attempted to downplay his disability and get around it as much as possible.

"It really wasn't an issue," George insisted. "No one ever took me aside to talk about it. I never got reprimanded for it."

He had his own team of soldiers working on his behalf, yet those soldiers were not trained in his battleground. The home team included Mom and Grandma, and they likely did much of his homework for him (parents of even literate children do that now). Of course they consoled him and praised him for everything he could do, and in the praising and doing of homework, he became a some-what spoiled little boy, expecting others to do his school work. This may have been a life-saving strategy, because he chose that path rather than the path of just giving up. He maintained his pleasant demeanor and personality through all of that.

His educational team at his school, St. Theresa, wasn't much better equipped for this type of disability. There wasn't much done to remediate his handicap, because as would be discovered later, he had a most serious form of dyslexia, and not much was known about dyslexia at the time, and the research about traumatic brain injury and its impact on reading acquisition hadn't yet been done. The sisters at St. Theresa had promoted him after keeping him two years in grade one and two years in grade three, and thankfully, they accommodated his handicap with teaching approaches, not knowing how else to help him. They just knew he needed help, and George knew how to endear himself to them.

"I was always very polite to the sisters. I knew how to become the teacher's pet. I volunteered for every job! My little girlfriend, Helen, was the smartest girl in the first grade. Once I made her mad at me, because I copied her spelling test. She had spelled one word wrong, but I copied that one wrong on my test, and I got it right! So I got a hundred percent that day, and she missed one. She told me, 'You can't get a better grade than me!'"

Was he ever not lucky?

CHAPTER 12

The Ernsts Decide to Move to Phoenix

WHILE SPUNKY WAS breezing through kindergarten class, George was struggling with the rigors of his second attempt at grade three, the year he should start reading to learn, not learning to read. He remained a "good" student, well behaved, and as always, the sister's pet. He made up as best he could for his lack of reading by being a good listener, absorbing much of what he needed to learn by paying attention to the teachers. He could do easy math—his numerical comprehension was good for adding and subtracting. Multiplication was a challenge.

But unbeknownst to him until Christmas of '44, he would be experiencing a consequential life change during the school break. In the nearly freezing late fall of 1944, George's father had tired of the walk-around jobs he had held for ten years in Wilkes-Barre. Over several long-distance discussions with his friend Joe Banks, who had left Pennsylvania for Phoenix a few years earlier, George Sr. accepted a ticket from Joe to come out and see Arizona for himself.

"The place is ready to explode," Joe had said. "Guys from Luke Airfield are staying here after they get mustered out. Their wives are coming out and renting up all the apartments. You gotta come out here. There's all sorts of construction getting started. You had that electrical training—you're a shoo-in for work. Plus, it's fun here. There's real-life Indians walking around, real cowboys on horses riding around, and saguaro cactuses everywhere."

That was an incentive?

"And it's warm!"

That was an incentive.

Within days of being in the beautiful early winter climate of Phoenix at Joe's behest, George Ernst Sr. called his wife and said, "Sell the house, sell the car. Come as soon as you can." Ever obedient, Mom agreed to move from her lifelong hometown to a state that was still considered western and wild so her husband could move into a different line of work. His early electrical training would pay off.

The family prepared to leave their extended family, so important to them, take their first airplane ride, and relocate to a totally different clime and culture. A wife would do what a husband would ask. Whither thou goest and all that. George just wanted to see his dad, to get to wherever he was. He missed him and wasn't used to having him gone. Leaving his friends and even his grandparents didn't matter. He missed his dad. And he would get to ride on an airplane!

"Great! Let's do it!" was George's emphatic reply.

CHAPTER 13

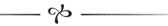

The Airplane Ride and Hotel Adventure

GEORGE'S PARENTS HAD finally given him a baby brother two years earlier in Pennsylvania. George didn't think it would ever happen! Most of his cousins had kid brothers or sisters—now he did too. And then right after they arrived in Phoenix, Mrs. Ernst produced another child, this time a girl, Mary! In fact, she had been pregnant with Mary on the trip out to Phoenix on Trans World Airlines, which may have played a part in Marian's overprotective and emotional nature on a stopover in Philadelphia. There was an unplanned stopover due to weather, and TWA provided a hotel for the passengers on the flight to Phoenix. It was a nice hotel, several stories high, with bellhops and room service. Marian was pregnant and traveling on her first flight with two children, George and his two-year-old brother. After getting to their hotel room, she decided to call for room service for her hungry kids. Soon, she heard the knock on the door and opened it with the chain on. She gasped, slammed the door, and immediately pushed the dresser over to the door to block whoever that person was from entering and harming her children. She ran to the phone and called downstairs, breathlessly whispering to the astonished desk clerk, "Hurry, get up here! The Japs have invaded us!" She created quite a melodramatic event in the room—children cowering in the closet, Mom scurrying.

"Ma'am, he works here. He's one of the interned Japanese that we hired after they were released. He's the bellhop with room service."

Holy Mary Mother of God.

CHAPTER 14

First and Other Impressions

WERE THE ERNSTS disappointed on arrival in Phoenix to see that their new "rough" town was quite built up? It was an actual city as large as Wilkes-Barre, and they would need to drive out to the desert to see the cacti. They would be able to spot some Native Americans walking around downtown, but they were definitely in the minority by then.

Phoenix had been a relaxed, cosmopolitan, predominantly Anglo town for years, the Mexican influence noticeable only in certain sections of town, yes, across the tracks. Blacks were practically nonexistent except below Jefferson Street. Adult transplants from the East still looked like the East, the men wore suits and ties to work, and the women wore dresses, heels, and stockings to walk about town.

The Ernsts were wise to come in early 1945, before the fellows started coming back from overseas and Japan. They couldn't have found a home if they had waited a year or two more. With the help of their friend Joe Banks, who was also Georgie's godfather, they found temporary housing at first and a delightful home just north of Roosevelt Street on Twenty-Fourth Place not long after. They were a few miles east of downtown but definitely part of the city energy; looking south, they could see the planes take off from Sky Harbor Airport. The streets in the area were still unpaved, the lots were large, and there was plenty of running room for kids and of course a dusty lot for pickup ball games. The residential lawns were irrigated with water from the nearest canal, a system initially designed by the Indians who lived in the valley more than two thousand years ago.

Dad took a job as an electrician, and Marian settled into the neighborhood, meeting everyone. She loved her new home—no one else lived there with them, there were no stairs and no basement, and she had fourteen mature trees on the property from which she could hang her hammock. She loved it when the irrigation water would flow underneath her, one day every other week. If George wanted to get on her good side for the day, all he had to do was volunteer to push his mom in the hammock. "Georgie, you know you are my favorite boy, don't you? Because your little brother isn't big enough to push me, is he?"

The Ernsts saw their first Indians (a few), cowboys (some), irrigation (a lot), Mexicans (quite a few), and Mormons.

"There were lots of Mormons in our neighborhood. They had dances at their ward, and everybody was invited. Everyone got along just fine," George remembered.

Socially, George would be fine—there was plenty for a boy to do around his neighborhood as well as a few miles out.

"In the summer we swam in the canal, about a mile away at Thirty-Second Street and Roosevelt. Yes, that's right. I know adults frowned on that, but we could do it. Little kids played in the irrigation ditches that watered the lawns. If we wanted to play on the huge tractor inner tubes, we got a parent to drive us over to Nelson's Pool on Nineteenth Avenue. It only cost a dime to get in, and that water was cold," George said.

Catholic Mass

The first thing Marian did after getting the suitcases into the temporary housing was *get her family to church*! George Jr. had by then seen enough of the neighborhood boys to realize that they dressed differently out here than back home. So when Mom laid out his knickers and white shirt and tie on Sunday, he enlightened her. "Oh no, Mom. The boys don't wear those out here. They all wear Levi's and T-shirts! I haven't even seen any knickers out here at all."

"George, you can bet they don't wear those Levi's to Mass. Put your knickers on."

He wasn't happy, but he did it. And at St. Agnes Church that morning, it was clear that George had been right and Mom was not this time. Some of the boys wore dress pants or khakis, but most had on denim jeans. There wasn't a pair of knickers in sight. He was mortified. I suspect his prayer life suffered that day. And Mom? Well, she came through. When they got in the car to go home, she turned to him and said, "George, you'll never have to wear knickers again."

CHAPTER 15

Spunky's Wild Ride

MEANWHILE, RIGHT THERE in Arizona, a hundred miles away from George, Spunky was also having adventures.

Miners usually like to drink. Wouldn't you? Think of the sparkling cool relief of a cold brew going down after a long day of digging copper out of the ground in, most of the time, really hot Arizona. Ask Roberto Jaurequi, Spunky's dad. He had the miner's propensity to drink hard on the weekends and make of it a good time—if you could call it that.

One weekend day when Spunky was just a little girl, her father and Mr. Leopold, the German boarder the Jaurequis had taken into their new hotel, decided after having a few brews in the local tavern to take a drive over to Dewey by way of old Highway 89A and the Old Black Canyon Highway and do a little more drinking. It was still daytime, and Arizona's summer sunshine lasted until 8:00 p.m., so OK—why not take a couple of children along for the ride?

That would have been questionable on the face of it, as it was a very long drive over a winding mountain road, much of it dirt. They rounded up Spunky, about six or seven, and her cousin Ruben, about the same age. Had Momma sent her daughter along to keep an eye on Dad, just in case he forgot he was married?

Whatever. The ride up was uneventful; the time in Dewey was absolutely boring for the kids. There was one street and nothing for them to do. They were kept outside of the bar where Dad and Mr. Leopold were drinking. Their boredom led to hunger. There's no telling how long they waited for the men to emerge from the bar and whether they ever got fed, but it was long enough for both the driver and passenger to get pretty damn drunk. By now in today's world, the men would have been arrested for child endangerment.

The adventure would get worse. Eventually, and of course by now in the dark, the men departed to make their way up to and back across the mountain on the narrow, winding dirt road. And they were drunk. The kids could tell because the car was tipping back and forth, left to right. It's not like the car could weave—the road wasn't wide enough for that. So the corrections in driving had to be made in short little starts and stops by pulling the steering wheel over quickly and tapping the brakes when necessary. They were going at a snail's pace, but how could the children know they wouldn't crash into another car or drive off the side of the road?

They were frightened. They sat frozen in the back seat of the old four-door Chevy and clenched their fists. They barely looked at each other. They nearly cried. And finally, Ruben looked across at Spunky and said, "Spunky, I'm gonna jump out."

She responded, "Me too."

And they did.

Meeting up a bit down the road, they were unhurt and knew what to do. They could see the lights of a little house several yards across the way and ran there. The residents of the house notified the sheriff, and soon the children were transported home, and the men were located and taken to the jailhouse in Prescott. Her father pleaded his innocence: "Officer, we tried to find those kids!"

Cousin Ralph came from Jerome and bailed the errant men out.

CHAPTER 16

—— ❦ ——

Oh Boy, School

OF COURSE, GEORGE would have to go to school. And how would that go, in a new state and new system—public, not parochial, with no nuns to nurse him through it—starting in the middle of the school year in a grade two grades below his age group? Would a helpful girl be available, and would she be pretty? Would there be *anyone* willing to help him? With these concerns surely in the back of his mind—or the forefront—George started the second half of grade four at age eleven at Creighton Elementary on McDowell Road, a mile away from home. He could walk to school, just as he had done in Wilkes-Barre. What would he encounter in this new school?

In fourth grade, Mrs. Krauss's class, children could already read and write paragraphs. Would the teacher have the kids read the stories and history lessons out loud, like they did in Wilkes-Barre? Had his parents met with the teachers and principals at the new school to alert them to the fact that he could *not* read, other than a few words in little books such as first-graders read? Were they ready for him?

Yes, Marian had met with the school prior to his first day in class, and the school's response was appropriate and professional. The teacher probably listened to him fumble aloud in class while trying to read his turn; then she may have asked him to come up to her desk and read to her while the others were out of the room at recess. She most likely told him he didn't need to read aloud and she would skip him when the rest of the class did so. The teacher knew it was bad—he couldn't even write much more than his name. Her apprehension of trying to impart the curriculum to this new boy was most likely palpable. She waited only a few days to take action to get George assessed for reading and writing deficiencies. The school psychologist administered a standardized reading test; George scored three years below the norm for his grade, a nearly irreparable lag in reading ability, at least in the days before specialists were trained to remediate. The test administrator noted on the report that he had a "good attitude." They immediately placed him in a remedial reading class, which was a precursor to the special-education classes that would be federally mandated in 1975 but were nonexistent or rare before that. At the end of the school year, a full-scale academic evaluation was administered, and he scored two years behind his fourth-grade peers across the board when his scores over reading, math, writing and general knowledge were averaged for a full-scale score (remember, he should have been in grade five or six by now). The test included oral responses to questions about concepts (e.g., why is the sky dark at night) and facts (What is this in the picture—a tree, a plant or a flower?) that students would have acquired in school and at home. That section of the test brought his general knowledge score to a reasonable level, thus raising the average score on the test to only two grades behind his peers. Because unrelated to his inability to read and write, he could learn and remember. He wasn't mentally slow. He was damaged.

The Ernsts may have hoped that a public-school education would make a difference and the teachers would teach him better. Perhaps he would grow out of it in a different state. And maybe pigs would fly.

There were no sisters to protect and coddle him, but Mrs. Krauss knew how to help him learn. "George," Mrs. Krauss instructed, "when the others read, you just listen, and listen good. And always ask questions! You will learn from your questions."

And he did. When teachers asked questions about the lesson, he would raise his hand and answer—right or wrong. And then he would ask a "what," "why," or "how" question.

He had to at least participate—he was a survivor, self-taught. He didn't know why he couldn't read or write—it was a mystery to him. In fact, he could memorize a few words, but on his permanent school record under "Written Expression," the teacher had written, "None." What an immense burden for a child of modern-day America.

Yes, there was a pretty girl in the class, and yes, she helped him as much as possible. Her name was Jane Carlisle. Unfortunately, his outgoing behavior was not as welcome in this school as it had been in St. Agnes Catholic School. On the "Comments" section of his year-end report card, the teacher had written, "Bothers others." This is not uncommon with children who struggle in school. They are bored, they are trying to pass time, and they are hoping to distract attention from their disability by entertaining others. Another remark the teacher made under the category of "Classroom Behavior" was "Fair."

Soon, George and Marian Ernst were filled with the same dread and apprehension regarding George as they had been in Wilkes-Barre.

"He's not learning. This is getting desperate, Marian. What's wrong with him? He's smart enough."

Marian was as concerned. "Let's try a tutor. I'll ask at the school for some names. We have to try something. His teachers have tried everything."

And so they found a tutor. Marian drove him to a tutor in Sunnyslope, five miles away from their home. After several months of instruction, even the tutor had to tell them she couldn't figure it out; she couldn't help him remember the sounds the letters made, let alone words. He couldn't spell. He absolutely couldn't learn. Maybe another tutor could do it.

─────── ✿ ───────

CHAPTER 17

Roosevelt Dies

WHAT A YEAR was 1945. George changed states and schools, and not long after, the beloved president of the United States died. Franklin Roosevelt had been elected for an unprecedented fourth term in November of 1944 as president of the United States, even as he appeared to be dying. No one wanted to unload the end of the tragic war onto a neophyte candidate, and Roosevelt wanted to be in the bird seat for the making of the peace that would come. D-day had essentially assured that. Too many young Americans had been killed in battle, and too many cities and towns had been destroyed in Europe. The world seemed to be in tatters. Roosevelt didn't want to watch the repairs from any seat but the highest seat in the land. Though he didn't know it, it would be his near-final and most enduring political act when he replaced his vice president with a quiet but determined little senator from the state of Missouri, Mr. Harry Truman.

No death since the assassination of President Lincoln had made such an impact on the American public. The president of the United States died in office of a massive cerebral hemorrhage—a stroke—on April 12 while vacationing with his most beloved mistress and other female friends and assistants. The country mourned. The world mourned. His wife even mourned, but she carried on.

On the day after the death, the front pages all across America and much of the world were covered with twenty-four-inch headlines of the death and smaller headlines about the new president, Harry S Truman. The *Arizona Republic* chose to use all capital white block letters on a black banner, "PRESIDENT DIES," and below that, they made the same mistake that many others would by putting a period after his middle initial: "Harry S. Truman Takes Oath As 33rd President of US."

Across the page in larger type was the good news that "Army Says Victory Is Close."

And squished prominently between those two articles was the local story that surely was a relief to most Phoenicians and their children: "Rodeo Plan Unchanged by Death."

On that eventful and historical day, the radios all over America were abuzz when the death of FDR was announced. Word had gone out to everyone at work and at home, and Jerome was no exception—and so the miners' wives had stopped their housecleaning and cooking to sit down in shock at the news, as did George's mother and father 110 miles away in Phoenix. The miners would hear the news when they returned home after their tedious day in the open pit; their wives and children would barrage them with information. School teachers would cry silently, and some would even weep if they were especially fond of the president. All would be respectful. Very few Americans didn't care. FDR had talked them through the Second World War with fatherly concern and strength.

George would have been eleven years old, and Spunky, six. As a kindergarten student who had turned six in February, she might have wondered which president had died—was it the man in the funny white wig, the skinny one with the beard and sad eyes, or the man who talked to them on the radio every week? She would have felt the sadness of her teacher and later on that day the sadness of her mother. George might have been especially concerned with the issue; Grandpa had talked about the war and the president so often. How would he take it?

CHAPTER 18

— ❧ —

Young Adolescent Life, Including Work

By the end of the fifth grade, George was twelve in a class of peers who were ten and eleven. He was pubescent and "bothering others." Grades six and seven were about the same as grade five—Ds and Fs—but his PE grades were good, as athletics were becoming his bailiwick and his compensation. Competitive sports gave him the self-esteem he needed on the ball and track fields, and he was collecting blue ribbons for first place.

So how did George manage to get promoted from the eighth grade? The practice of social promotion—promoting students based on their age and size-- was by this time becoming established, at least in Phoenix and other towns where there were no coal mines for which young men were destined. Educators were beginning to understand that some reading and writing problems were the result of a learning dysfunction or (as it would eventually be diagnosed) a learning disability. The inability to read or write wasn't always, or even usually, a result of an intellectual disability. Even with the help he received and the lack of censure by the teachers or students, by now the insecurity and anxiety associated with failure in the classroom were eroding his behavior at school and creating a misbehaving boy.

Seems about right. Kids who can't read have a lot of downtime in school. It's harder for nonreaders to get a lot out of the seven-hour day. Often, they become bored and must think of ways to entertain themselves, usually by entertaining classmates. Often they get comments on their report cards that say, "Poor work habits" and

"Poor effort." Ignorant teachers will say, "Poor use of time," and they'll tell the student *and* his parents that "if he would just spend the time he wastes fooling around *applying* himself…"

His parents tried another tutor with the same results. By now, George was going into the sixth grade; he was thirteen years old and taller than the rest of the kids in his class. If he couldn't read by now, the teachers were becoming certain that he couldn't learn. They were right.

One day out of frustration, his teacher told George, "You just aren't learning to read as fast as you should." This seems reasonable and not too demeaning, but George was troubled by it and told his father what she had said.

Dad had to be frustrated as well, after all these years; he had tried to keep his concern between himself and his wife, but now it just came out. He growled but clearly enough said, "You'll probably never learn how to read."

Mom was mortified, of course; she didn't know what to say, how to rebut that—he was thirteen or fourteen years old, and shouldn't he have learned better by now? At this point she really couldn't say, "Oh, sure you will, George." She was a reasonable person. So she didn't give him the reassurance she usually provided—all she could say was "George, that's just the way you are." And that was the first time his parents ever made him cry. He still feels the pain of his parents' disappointment more deeply than the pain of illiteracy.

But the rest of his world—his home life, his work life, his social life—was satisfying. And in these arenas, he remained his pleasant, happy, endearing self. And resourceful, as we have seen when he decided to join the US Navy.

George Compensates

"George," I asked, "I really need to ask you one more time. How did your reading disability affect you as you got older? How did you feel about it when you moved to Phoenix and started a new school?"

"I really didn't think it was an issue. I don't think anyone knew— maybe the teachers did, but not the kids...no one ever teased me about it. I always outdid everyone else in sports, because I was older and a bit bigger. No one took me aside to talk to me about it; I just got by."

It was clear from his ongoing records and testing results that unbeknownst to George, or forgotten by him, his teachers and the school administration definitely knew, and to the credit of the teachers there, he may have felt that he was doing OK. That's good teaching.

"And I was very polite, and my teachers liked me," George added.

George found plenty to do besides look for someone to help him complete his homework assignments. Besides his paper route, he babysat for the next-door neighbors. His mom helped him with any reading and writing related to tossing the paper or caring for the children. Disabilities create self-preservation strategies and resourcefulness in people that some of us without them don't develop.

An example is the way he figured out how to play football without a ball. He had made a best friend when he was eleven and new to Phoenix. He and Bill Cramer bonded over football, playing around in the neighborhood. Between the two of them, they couldn't buy a football, so they improvised. They took socks (likely those with holes in them) and formed a football out of them. It wasn't likely that George would ever need professional football equipment, as by the time he was old enough to join the navy, he weighed only 140 pounds.

Interscholastic sports saved him. By thirteen years of age, George had matured into an athletic kid who could play ball and run. He didn't need to invent clever ways to win at sports—he was just good. It helped that he was one of the tallest kids in class, being two years older than most. And to get and stay good, he practiced and worked hard at games and winning—he liked all those blue ribbons hanging on his bedroom wall. He was an all-star in middle school, and of course, that didn't hurt with the girls. Now a preteen, he would need some success in his life to figure out who he was and who he was going to be. Would he be a kid easily drawn into a life of petty crime, a dejected loner who couldn't fit in, or would he be a contributing member of society with the emotional stamina to construct a successful life in spite of a debilitating handicap?

Fortunately, he knew how to defend himself if necessary. One time on the playground, a group of boys who had been around longer than George met with him in a corner somewhat out of sight of the teacher on duty.

"Hey, four-eyes."

"What'd you say?"

"Hey, four-eyes."

"Are you sure you want to call me that?"

"Yeah. Yeah, I do, four-eyes."

"OK. I'll whip your ass for that." And so he took off his glasses and set them on the ground. "C'mon," he challenged them.

The antagonist came at him with his fists, and George *did* whip his ass, and as the punk was lying on the ground, one of the other bullies ran over and crushed George's glasses with his foot. By then, adults had joined the fray and broke up the fight. George went home and got in trouble because his glasses were hopelessly broken.

"What happened here?" hollered George Sr.

"Dad, he called me names. I warned him I'd beat him up. He said, 'Fine,' so I put my glasses on the ground, and I punched him a few times."

"You *what*? George, damnit, glasses cost money!"

"I know, Dad, sorry. I'll pay for a new pair with my paper-route money."

George Sr. steamed and fumed for a few minutes, thinking. "No, George, but *next time,* hand your glasses to a friend!"

Newspapers and Winnie Ruth

Ironically, as a young teen he took a job delivering a product he would never use—the *Phoenix Gazette,* afternoon sister paper to the *Arizona Republic.* His work would take him to an interesting locale quite close to his home—the Arizona State Mental Hospital on Twenty-Fourth Street and Van Buren. In those days, there was a famous resident in a special unit that could be accessed by the paperboy and probably others. This resident worked in the hospital beauty shop, alongside her mother, who also worked in the beauty shop. The patient was Winnie Ruth Judd, and she had committed a horrific crime—two murders—with help, of course. So many people in Phoenix believed that she had killed in self-defense and had been railroaded and set up by some wealthy doctors and their friends to take the rap for dissecting the bodies that she wasn't considered a risk, except by some hysteria-prone children. George wasn't one of them. He liked Winnie Ruth and got to talk to her frequently when he delivered the *Gazette* to the hospital beauty shop. But even better, he got to see her when she occasionally escaped from the hospital and ran down his street, which was just south of the mental hospital, to a secret safe house. When anyone escaped (and it was usually Winnie), the hospital would ring an alarm that could be heard for blocks and blocks around. When that happened, George's mother would call out to him, "Georgie, get some milk. Winnie Ruth has escaped." He'd get the milk out of the icebox and shake it up to get the cream mixed in, and within minutes she would run by the house and he would hold out a bottle of cold milk for her.

"Thanks, George. Watch out for my mom. They'll catch up with me in a couple of months, and I'll be back."

"She loved milk," George recalled.

It has always been assumed that Winnie Ruth had help escaping and hiding. Perhaps there were several compassionate neighbors along the way who made sure she got what she needed. The Ernsts would have been some of those Good Samaritan neighbors.

Young Love on the Paper Route

Customers on his route thought the world of George. That personality, that charm, that sweetness, those manners—these attributes came across on the job. He was a trusted kid in the neighborhood. Young parents asked him to babysit their children, his customers would come outside to grab the paper from him if they were home, and some even went to his house and picked up their paper when it was raining. He not only earned the route salary for delivering 120 papers Monday through Friday afternoons, he also earned tips. And there was a cute young girl his age. He remembers he said, "Mom, is it OK if I have a girlfriend on the route? Her name's Mary Lou. She's awful nice, and she's fun. I met her on the route, on Culver Street. Don't worry—she's Catholic!"

"George, just don't forget your mom, and remember to be a gentleman! And don't go in her house if her folks aren't there. How old is she?"

Mary Lou's family lived in a small brick house as neat and clean as was possible given that they had no mother. Mary Lou and her sister Gina took care of the house. The grass was always mowed; the house was painted; the old car stayed washed and maintained. Inside, although the place was neat, the family was in turmoil. Mary Lou confided in George, "My dad drinks too much." She was embarrassed to let George in the house later in the evening if her dad was there—that's when the drinking occurred—but he could come in after school because Dad would be home and sober after his shift at the Holsum Bakery on Grand Avenue. George could tell when her father was home—the fragrance of the bread clung to his clothes and his body until he showered.

"You smell like bread, Mr. Kelly. Have some butter?" George would tease anyone.

It's not easy for thirteen-year-olds to talk about their parents' drinking, but George was easy to talk to. He shared with her his illiteracy. They had a bond; they each had a secret burden, and they had each other. One day, he went by the house, and her dad came out.

"Mary Lou's not feeling well today, George. She had a dentist appointment earlier, and she's feeling punk."

That wasn't the end of it. She felt worse and worse, and by the end of the week, she was at the doctor's office with a raging infection in her jaw.

"She's got a bad one, Mr. Kelly," the doctor said. "I'm going to admit her to Good Samaritan Hospital. This infection seems to have progressed to her blood."

And so the sweet friend with whom George experienced his first serious love was hospitalized for weeks. He would visit every Wednesday night, and they would watch the fights on the TV in the lobby. He'd pretend to be a boxer, bouncing around the small room, and she would laugh. He would have been a bantamweight, if that. They enjoyed each other. They were friends.

And then she was gone.

"Where'd she go?" he asked.

When his mother told him, he cried. How could this happen? How could she die from the dentist? This patient had died as a result of poor dental practices of the day—dentists didn't wear gloves, and the instruments were poorly sanitized. And a piece of George's heart had broken. He couldn't let go of the family; he remained a casual friend of her sister Gina, but he didn't get any more chances to ask her dad if he had any butter.

George kept his paper route until the end of the eighth grade. As a paperboy, he had been exposed to the depths of despair which some families endured (unlike his). The Kellys were one, and sadly, the Kellys' next-door neighbor, also a customer of George's, was another. He was a police officer who took care of his severely mentally disabled daughter; eventually he couldn't handle the stress of it and took his own life. And remember, George met and conversed with a person decreed criminally insane by the state of Arizona, perhaps the most famous Arizonan in that category then or now. All of these people meant more to George than just owners of yards at which to throw papers; he sympathized and cared about their lives.

At the same time, the job he did not only brought him the self-worth his academic life could not, but it also brought spending money of his own, the great motivator, and of course the work ethic, which would help him develop into the kind of person who could depend on himself as an adult—literate or not.

CHAPTER 19

High School

AFTER TEN YEARS in K–8 schools, he matriculated with a diploma. He was fifteen years and eleven months old. The conundrum became "What is George going to do for high school?" His parents, the teaching staff, and George himself determined that the Phoenix Union Technical School electrical course would be the best course for him. He would play football on the first team and earn his letter in his freshman year.

"Will I have to read to do electrical work?" He was concerned.

His father tried to reassure him. "Some. But you'll get by just like you always have, George. You'll have everyone else read it for you, and your mom and I will do your homework!"

His father planned to get him into the electrician's union after he finished a two-year tech-school course. No one expected him to go on to regular classes after that. George could then apprentice under his father. It seemed so obvious to George Sr., but Jr. was not so sure he wanted to be a ward of his father all his life.

It wasn't easy to just get socially promoted out of Phoenix Technical School.* Employers in Phoenix considered the school a reliable and good source of blue-collar workers. Students were graded on their skills, work ethic, and aptitude for specific trades. The report card at the end of his first high school year stung both George Sr. and Jr.

"George, what the *hell*! OK, so you can't read! Is that any excuse for a 'poor' on 'job judgment'? And 'attitude'? Son, your attitude had better improve next year! Do you want to get that driver's license or not?" His dad had been tutoring him on how to answer the questions on the test and how to get the test administrator to help him. He had long ago reached the age he had to be to get his learner's permit.

He begged, "Dad, I don't wanna go back to school! I want to join the navy now, not later! I'm seventeen…you could sign for me."

That didn't happen.

During that second year, his job performance mark did improve from "poor" to "fair," as his dad had insisted. But "attitude" stayed "poor," and even his "health" and "personal appearance" marks went from "excellent" to just "good." George was exhibiting a classic case of depression. His natural resourcefulness was starting to fail him. His self-care was suffering. What would it take to get him out of school? George remembers it in a more positive light, "It was mostly hands-on—volts meter, how to wire a house, stuff like that." His grades suggest otherwise.

Dad had a plan to give George a sense of accomplishment, a plan that would provide the experience of a lifetime and help him develop those skills other than academics which he would need to succeed.

And he would need that driver's license. Everyone in Phoenix of driving age had a license. How would he take the test?

* Phoenix Technical School became a member of the Phoenix Union High School District in 1956.

CHAPTER 20

—— ❦ ——

Must-Have Transportation

GEORGE ERNST SR. was definitely the type of man that trained up a son in the ways of manliness, as defined by that which is potentially dangerous, that which demands self-defense, and that which would not tolerate a helicopter parent. After a few years in Phoenix and a few years of frustrating school life for his son, he befriended men of the community who were also of the manly ilk—including bankers, lawyers, and businessmen, some of whom were good with horses and who were developing a popular annual event together with some local guys up in Williams, Arizona, eventually to be known as the Bill Williams Mountain Men. The men participating in the event started in Williams and rode horseback down through the mountains and valleys and arroyos of central Arizona, Prescott, and then Phoenix to participate in the Jaycee Rodeo of Rodeo Parade every March. One of George Sr.'s friends happened to have a workhorse that might be a good starter horse for George.

"George, I've got you set up with the fellows riding down from Williams for the Rodeo Parade this year, which means you'll be getting a horse of your own. You'll start in Prescott—Joe'll drive you and your horse up there in the trailer."

"OK, Dad, but you know I've never even been on a horse before."

"Won't matter, George. It'll be a slow ride over several days. You're thirteen—old enough. There might be a couple of other boys your age. Not sure."

And so George met—and named—Tommy, his first horse. Tommy was just a cow pony, and it was the first time George had ever been on a horse, so it was a long ride on a slow horse. The men and two or three other teenage boys would stop and camp out on the way; they'd sit around the fireplace at night and tell stories, eat beans, and pass gas. The trip took less than a week, and for a sixteen-year-old boy, it was heaven, especially since George was allowed to stay out of school for the week. When they arrived in downtown Phoenix, some of the guys rode right into the lobby of the Adams Hotel on Central Avenue and then on to the parade and thousands of adoring onlookers.

George went the next year, too. He had an old army saddle, a cow pony, and a great aptitude for adventure. He boarded his horse at a house with horse property down the street from his home. Between his two Mountain Man rides, he and the horse managed to get in trouble.

"When I had my horse, we snuck into the hay bales one night in the Chinese family's barn and stole a bale of hay. My horse dragged it home for me. It started with a hay fight. It was at night, and Bill and Joe and I snuck into the barn at the Huang family home down the street from us. We got in there and started picking out the hay from the bales and tossing it at each other, and it turned into a pretty good fracas.

"The next morning, I was asleep, and the police came to the house. The family was convinced I was the guy, and they had evidence. Of course I denied it, told my folks, 'No, Mom, Dad—I wouldn't do that, you know that.'"

"Where's your evidence, Officer?" asked his dad.

"Come with me, Mr. Ernst. Look down the street, here."

"And there was the evidence, a long line of hay from the Huang house to our house. I had to pull a lot of goat heads that week as a punishment. I never felt so bad in my life about hurting my parents. We kinda knew the family—not well, but my mom knew almost everyone on the block. She wasn't too happy with me that day. I let them down and disappointed them. I never forgot that.

"I kept Tommy, my horse, for another year and for another Mountain Man ride. He was the best. He couldn't read, either."

From a Horse to a Car!

"Mom, Dad—I'll be old enough to get my learner's permit next month. Can I get it? I need it, Dad."

And after his father helped him with the test, he did get it. He was now working as an electrician's apprentice and starting to think about dating. He had made it through the tenth grade, and although he would miss his football-playing days, he would not miss school. He had improved his "job performance" grade; that's what Dad had insisted on. But getting a license would involve more than just keeping his car in his lane and parallel parking; there was a written test.

Driving in Phoenix was an absolute must in the '50s and '60s, especially for teenage boys, to impress the girls. And commuters needed it. For all intents and purposes, there was little to no public transportation for workers and shoppers living outside the city core. Bus lines ran on the hour most of the day and the half hour during peak traffic times. Phoenix and the surrounding small towns were all driving meccas; the Mormons had designed the town of Mesa on a square grid with wide four-lane streets and avenues unbridled with sidewalks until the '50s, and Phoenix had followed suit. Boys could drop their fathers off at work and drive their behemoth Fords and Chevys to school or buy old clunkers of their own with the money they saved from their after-school jobs.

How could George get his driver's license? He applied for it years before the state of Arizona started helping Spanish speakers, and yes, nonreaders, pass the written exam. When he was sixteen, in 1950, applicants were expected to pass the test by themselves. George and his father had devised a strategy based on how George had been learning for all these years—by asking questions and discussing the topic. "Just keep talking!" his mom had advised him early on.

He practiced with his dad, and on the day he took the test, he presented himself to the clerk at the window as a polite, compliant young man. He took the test sheet to his desk, looked it over carefully, and started to check a box. Then he approached the clerk at the window again. Pointing at a word, he said, "Sir, I don't quite understand this question. Can you explain it? Because I see it as [this way], and this question makes me wonder if I should see it [this other way]...what do you think? Because when I was reading the book, it seemed that it meant [this way]."

Basically, he wore the guy out with questions on several test items and chatter, until the fellow just said, "Let's read this together!" He probably was thinking, "Let's get this kid outta here!"

─────── ⚵ ───────

CHAPTER 21

Lessons from Mom and Dad

George Sr.

A TYPICAL DAD tries to teach his kids about the value of a dollar. George Sr. was typical and had been teaching his son about the importance of a dollar for his whole life. (It's been said that he was actually a tightwad.) He wasn't totally unreasonable; he could prioritize his financial values, as he had that day George's glasses were broken by placing his son's right to defend himself over the expense of a new pair of glasses.

Good Dad.

Another lesson occurred in which Dad's priorities were questionable. George Jr. had been delivering the *Phoenix Gazette* for several months when his mother's birthday drew near. George adored his mom and had saved his money to spend on a special gift. She had talked about the new electric skillets being advertised on TV and on display at J. C. Penney's department store. He knew she wanted one. Of course she did! She was a modern mom. So on the day he had enough money saved, he rode his bike downtown and bought the bright-yellow electric skillet. He was proud of his gift—he loved his mom.

However, the gift didn't go over well at home with Dad, the electrician. Before George could even present the gift to his mother, his father hit the roof.

"George! What are you trying to do?! Come out here, boy."

Whereupon he dragged George and his skillet out by the ear, metaphorically speaking, and stopped by the electric meter on the outside wall. Near it was an outlet, where Dad plugged in the soon-to-be-maligned modern appliance.

"Watch this, George. Watch this needle go." And George did watch it, and the needle did go, nearly wild, indicating a huge surge in use of electricity from plugging in the skillet.

George was saddened and yet nonplussed. "But, Dad, it'll make Mom's work easier..."

And she got to keep the skillet.

Marian

When the family moved out from Wilkes-Barre to Phoenix, Marian had never lived anywhere else, so she was going to move slowly into social life—or what she knew of it. She focused on the neighbors first and befriended them and fit in easily. Initially, though, she had a steep learning curve about George's new denim-wearing friends. He, of course, made quick friends and lots of them. One day a kid asked George for a glass of water before he left for home on his bike. George brought him into the kitchen and introduced him to his mom. Marian was gracious if wary—these Arizona boys seemed a bit wild—but filled a glass for him. After he left her kitchen, she put the glass he had used in a towel and hit it against the sink, breaking it into pieces.

"Mom! Why did you do that?!"

"Georgie, we don't know if he has anything!"

CHAPTER 22

— ✿ —

The Union, the Smoker, and the Birds and the Bees

As WARNED AND promised, when George left his formal education after doing poorly in tenth grade, George Sr. reminded him of his plan.

"George, you are going to be an electrician. I can get you into the union and help you pass the test. You passed your driver's test! You need a skill, a real profession. You're too small to be a laborer. Come on. You took the course at Phoenix Tech. You can do it."

George was skeptical. He knew that he hadn't been able to hack the electrical course at Phoenix Tech. Dad was still living in a dream world and trying to protect his son. George Sr. was now a small-business owner in a different field, but he still had the connections to help George get an apprenticeship under the electricians installing wire at the Newberry's five-and-dime store downtown.

"It was easy. My job was to lay down gold leaf between two pieces of copper," George recounted.

George didn't want his dad to be the one taking care of him, and George wanted to chart his own course. But right now he didn't have a choice, and not wanting to appear ungrateful to his father, George went along with the plan to get him into the union, just until he could join the navy. It wasn't bad; the journeymen liked him. After the Newberry's job, he was kept busy installing an alarm system for the J. C. Penney department store downtown. Working with those grown men, actual electricians, taught him a lot—including about the facts of life.

George was sixteen and working in the electrical field when he learned about the birds and the bees, and not from his father. Well, sort of from his father. Oh, sure, he'd heard stuff from the guys at school; he had kissed a girl or several—but he was in for the education of his life when he heard some older guys from work talking about a "smoker" they had planned for the weekend.

"What's a smoker, guys?"

"Ha ha! Why don't you come and find out?"

"I might."

On the night of the smoker, George was getting ready to go, dressing up in his blue jeans and white T-shirt and combing his hair. His dad came by his room and asked, "What are you gonna do this weekend, George?"

"I'm going to a smoker, Dad. Do you want to go with me?"

At that, George Sr. kind of sputtered a bit and declined, but his mother insisted, "Go with him, George."

Right about then, Dad was probably thinking, "Why haven't I told him anything yet? Do I hafta?" Yes, Senior, you probably should. Otherwise, he's gonna end up at that "smoker" and come out reeling from shock. Man up.

"George, look, it's hard to say, exactly, but well…it's dirty movies. Look—ah geez, I'll tell you what—you can't go to the smoker alone, but I'll go with you. You're seventeen—not a kid anymore."

Not only George Jr. but George Sr. came out of the smoker reeling. "George, you can't tell anyone about this."

At that point, Mr. Ernst told his son, "OK, George…as soon as you are finished with your apprenticeship, you can join the navy!"

Part 2

CHAPTER 23

— ✂ —

1953: In the Navy Now

FINALLY, IT WAS the right time for him to join the navy! That's what he had wanted to do all along; the navy was the branch he preferred. And the timing was right. At this point in US military history—but not for much longer—a man could sign up for unskilled positions in the armed services without taking a written test. Admittance forms were taken home. Up until now, George's good luck was mainly the result of his teachers and parents and friends, especially the pretty little girls in school with him who let him copy their papers.

He could have chosen the army. "Why did you choose the navy, George?" I asked him.

"The uniform. I liked all those buttons on the shirt, on the fly, on the cuffs. I was—and am—very fastidious. So the uniforms and the girls. Yes, I knew girls really liked sailors. And of course the ships attracted me. I liked everything about the navy."

Now would come the challenge of getting through any reading or writing assignments in basic training. Even though they hadn't been tested prior to enlisting, there would now be some literacy requirements. Would George serve a very short period and go home in disgrace?

Of course not! This is George, as well as his best friend Bill. Together they continued with their tandem test taking, like they had learned to do in elementary school. As George puts it, "I did a lot of copying."

Basic training in San Diego was over in six weeks—but not for George. He was kept another two weeks for specialized fire-safety training. Although no one alive knows this now, there must have been an officer defending George's usefulness to the navy's mission. Officers are not stupid (usually). They remain aware of their men's competence and know what's going on. George had something the navy wanted.

Bill and George were split up right away after basic training, and they wouldn't serve together at all. Bill was sent to the East Coast, and George was assigned out of Long Beach to the USS *Sunnadin*, ATA-197, an auxiliary fleet tug with ports of call at Pearl Harbor, Palmyra Island, and Johnston Island in Hawaii.

Without his accomplice, George would need to make new friends, and someone on board would need to know about his inability to read and write while on active duty. Fortunately, he made the acquaintance of a yeoman in personnel known by the nickname "Buttons." Yeomen are the men who perform the administrative and clerical duties on a US naval ship. Buttons and George hit it off and became buddies. They wore the same size clothing and traded off, doubling their wardrobes, for off-base drinking and girl-hunting excursions. Buttons had surmised through their friendship that George didn't read or write very well. Out of curiosity, he went through George's personnel file. As a yeoman, he would have had access to do so. He saw a way he could help his friend.

"George, you don't even have a high school diploma! How are you gonna get a job when you get out of the navy with no diploma? Well, I will tell you how. No, I'll show you. Give me a few days on duty and I'll bring you one—for twenty-five dollars."

That's right. Buttons produced a high school diploma for George, just like the one he would have received from Phoenix Technical School. Was it luck or just good planning on George's part that brought these guys together?

While Buttons did a yeoman's work, George did the grunt work of sandblasting mothballed destroyers that were to be repainted.

He surely got enough of hard labor doing that, labor without the need to read or write.

Being in Long Beach was a real boon for a guy whose family lived in Phoenix. It was a six-hour drive between the two towns, and guys with a certain level of seniority were able to get the weekends off. Moreover, if they gave a pint of blood the preceding week, they could get off early on Friday. So, in uniform, George would finish his half day of sandblasting and hit the road, hitchhiking across the desert along Highway 8. He usually got home before sundown.

In Honolulu he got promoted to the position of electrician's mate, taking care of the two generators on the ship, switching them over from one to the other, and keeping the ship running, all of which sounds important. Pearl Harbor, Honolulu, was of course known for so much more than just a port of call, but it did have another distinction other than the attack by the Japanese in 1941. Because Hawaii wasn't yet a state, Honolulu didn't have a jail. Instead, it had a prison. And that's where George spent a full twenty-four hours for a DUI that could have been quite costly, but then again, this is George. Of course he got out of that.

The details of the event are murky, because George had been drinking—of course. This is the navy. And this is George. And we will see these events played out again later, because George will not always drink and drive with impunity. What happened in Hawaii, George?

"I was driving my friend's car there in Honolulu, after we had all been out drinking on a leave. Right downtown, I hit a Japanese guy's car—an actual resident of Hawaii, not an enemy. The damage wasn't too bad, but he was hot and kept yelling at me, saying what I thought was F. U.! The officers arrested me because I was obviously drunk. So they take me down to the prison—that's right, it was a prison, because at that time, Hawaii wasn't even a state—and shave my head. I got a prison number. Well, my chief petty officer bailed me out after a twenty-four-hour stay, because I was the property of the US government. He told me then, 'George, you have to keep your nose clean and stay off the streets. That guy is suing you for damages to his car. He wasn't saying, "F. U."; he was saying, "I'm going to *sue* you!"' He did try to sue me three months after I was out of the navy and back in Arizona at my folks' house. I get this official-looking letter with some attorney in Hawaii for the return address. My dad takes me out to the backyard and reads me the letter. The guy was trying to sue me, for sure. We called my dad's attorney friend, and he just laughed and said, 'George, don't ever go back to Hawaii. He can't touch you here.' And I didn't go back to Hawaii for forty years."

——— ✼ ———

CHAPTER 24

Meanwhile, Back in the States: Good-Bye to Jerome, Hello to High School

SPUNKY AND HER family had persevered in Jerome as a typical all-American family, pursuing the dual American dreams of a good education and small-business ownership. Spunky provided no surprises in school; she could read and write very well and was a good student. Meanwhile, her parents had purchased the small boarding-house next door to their home and turned one floor into a little restaurant for the boarders and other residents of Jerome; they called their establishment the Amigos Inn. Now Spunky's mom, Anita, had a full-time job in the hospitality business. She and Roberto were flourishing as hoteliers and restaurant owners, even as he continued to work in the mine. As Spunky grew up, her mother gave her more responsibility in the restaurant, having her help with table settings and clean and wash dishes. She was being instilled with the work ethic of her parents.

And then one day—it seemed to happen suddenly, when Spunky was to enter high school—there were no mines in Jerome or much of anything else other than two picturesque avenues of delightful homes and establishments. In 1953, Phelps Dodge closed their last mine on that mountain. The closure caused a mass exodus of the miners and most of the locals and left what would become Arizona's most famous ghost town. Residents moved down the hill to Clarksdale, Cottonwood, or further. Fortuitously, with the popularity of his wife's restaurant, Mr. Jaurequi had become a clever businessman. He had anticipated the mine closure and had secured a lease on restaurant space in Flagstaff at 114 S. San Francisco Street. A town much larger than Jerome, Flagstaff would provide many more potential customers for a Mexican food restaurant than Jerome or even Cottonwood. Jaurequi kept the name of the previous owner, so the Amigos Inn restaurant slipped seamlessly into Miguel's Diner. The green chili pork enchilada was an especial favorite of the gringos in town and those who traveled to "Flag" for the Snowbowl in the winter and the great hiking trails in the summer. Anita Jaurequi grew her own chilis in their garden and roasted them as needed for the dishes. Authenticity and flavor were the selling points for her restaurant. Roberto slipped comfortably into his new role as restaurateur.

Spunky Flourishes in High School

Spunky started high school in her new town, but many of her childhood friends and acquaintances were there with her because of the mass exodus from Jerome. Her after-school responsibilities hadn't changed; she worked the tables and washed dishes at the family diner, where she could get in some of her homework during the mid-afternoon downtimes. She had entered high school in September 1953, a month before George had entered the navy. While George had a painful high school experience, she flourished and was quite popular with her classmates.

"Mom! Guess who's the queen of hearts this year!"

"I wouldn't know, *mija.** Sounds like a card to me. Is it gambling?"

"Mom, it's the most popular girl in the school! It's me! And I get to be the queen of the Valentine's dance."

"Hmmm. Well, good for you. Better ask your dad if it's OK."

Her heart felt still. She felt that old feeling she had known growing up with her two older sisters, three and six years older than her. Mom had always seemed more interested in them. Her middle sister had catered to Mom and ingratiated herself to her. But surely Mom had enough love in her heart to be proud of Spunky for being selected as the queen of hearts as well as a cheerleader. She just didn't know how to show it.

An event occurred in her last year of high school that might have thrown a less resilient teenager into despair. During the last year of her parents' five-year lease on the building in Flagstaff, the miner-turned-businessman made a decision to build his own restaurant, ground up, down in the valley in the small town of Cottonwood. In most ways, this was astute, but for Spunky, not so much. This meant another move! This one would coincide exactly with Spunky's last year of high school. Fortunately, the little high school in Cottonwood was a branch of the Flagstaff Union High School, and so she graduated with the students she had attended with for four years, from the Flagstaff High School auditorium, with no adverse social or psychological ramifications. She just attracted more friends.

Of course she worked in the Cottonwood restaurant—the new Amigos Inn—and there she met some people who might have changed the trajectory of her life altogether. While waitressing, she was offered a job in Phoenix by a producer and his wife, both of whom worked for a movie production company. The movie *Twenty-Six Men* was filming in Flagstaff. This couple, their names long forgotten, managed the filming through the company, whose name will be withheld. They enjoyed many of their meals at the popular Amigos Inn and were impressed with Spunky's vivacious personality. They invited her to apply for an office job at their location in Cudia City when she graduated from high school. She would do so but not until after she graduated from high school and taken a year of business school. What would it be like to work for a movie studio, she wondered? She would find out.

* *Mija* is Spanish for "my daughter."

CHAPTER 25

Countdown to the Day They Finally Meet

In August 1957, George received an honorable discharge from the US Navy, armed with his phony high school diploma and a sense of accomplishment for a job well done. Before he disembarked the ship for the last time, Buttons approached George and said, "Hey, George. For an additional twenty-five dollars, let me know if you want a college diploma too!"

George realized the absurdity of that. "No, Buttons, I won't be needing a college diploma!" And George gave up his naval experience and flew back to Arizona, home to Mom and Dad. Home to some uncertainty. Now the real challenge of illiteracy would take on a deeper, more unsettling nature as he began working in the real world.

Three Months Earlier

In May '57, three months before George left the navy, Spunky finished basic training for her life's work. The commencement flyer for Flagstaff High School listed her as "Mary Helen Jaurequi, Business Studies." On graduation night, she walked boldly to the stage to accept her diploma, a petite yet powerful young lady, dark eyes blazing behind the square-rimmed glasses that lent an air of seriousness to her demeanor. Unlike George, whose future was uncertain, she knew what she wanted to do, and she had plans.

"Dad, I need to go to Lamson Business College in Phoenix. I can stay at the YWCA."

Lamson College was the best-known secretarial school in Arizona, and a girl who wanted a stellar education and resume would choose to go there. Although there was a Lamson College satellite in Flagstaff, Spunky wanted to go to the Phoenix campus. Perhaps she had a desire to see the world outside of her parents' perspective, and maybe she wanted to meet new people. In that respect, she had the same desire to spread her own wings as do most college students. But Señor Jaurequi was what we now would call über-strict. He had kept Spunky under his thumb throughout her teenage years; he saw no reason to lift that veil of protection just because she had turned eighteen.

"No, *mija.*"

"Please, Papa!" She played a better hand, suggesting she might stay with a family friend, Ramona.

"No."

"Please."

"Well," he relented, "we'll see if Ramona can give you a room. Otherwise, you are staying in Flagstaff."

Ramona opened her home to the eighteen-year-old, and so, for the first time, George and Spunky were in the same town! George was used to the big city of Phoenix, had been in the navy, had partied in Long Beach and Honolulu, had been arrested and thrown in prison, and had lived on a ship. Spunky, on the other hand, had lived in the little hamlet of Jerome and the small towns of Flagstaff and Cottonwood all her life. She wanted to meet new people, exercise her independence, and cut loose from the overprotectiveness of her father. Would this be the year she and George would meet? They would not be traveling in the same circles yet, but their paths were getting closer. Being safely ensconced under Ramona's matronly wing that year, Spunky kept to her studies and followed the house rules.

By October 1957, almost two months after George had returned, both were living in downtown Phoenix. She was in a neighborhood close to the barrio, and he was in his parents' home near downtown. She was attending business school to prepare herself for her life's work, and he was looking for a job, trying to not be dragged in by his father to continue as an electrician for life.

George's greatest challenge was on top of him now. How would he manage to secure work outside of the US Navy? How could he even qualify for a blue-collar job? Most decent-paying jobs required some reading and writing in order to fill out invoices and read instructions. George had expensive taste. He liked nice clothes and cars, and he liked women who appreciated those things. What could he do other than hard physical labor or work as an electrician's helper that would keep him in the lifestyle he preferred? Most guys with his extent of disability were unemployable, working in dead-end jobs, or wasting away in prison somewhere. Although George didn't know the statistics, they were brutal.*

Someone had told him that the phone company was hiring and that he wouldn't need to read anything. "Don't worry, George," his friend said, "phone installation is mostly a matter of color coding!" Just like electrical work! And once again, his luck, drive, and personality would ensure success. He made his appointment for the interview with the phone company. Of course, someone else, probably his mother, had filled out his job application, but he personally carried with him his beautiful, brand-new, never-been-used high school diploma. Now he would get a face-to-face interview with an actual personnel officer in a large utilities corporation. He sat down in the office of the interviewer. The fellow read as far as "birthplace" on George's application, smiled, and said, "I'm from Wilkes-Barre too! I came out here in 1950. What's your father's name?"

He didn't know George's father, but the conversation continued with talk of Wilkes-Barre and Pennsylvania.

"Do you have lots of family in Wilkes-Barre?" he was asked.

"Oh, about half the town!" joked George.

"Any doctors?"

"Sure. Uncle Frank and Uncle Karl."

"Jesus, Mary, and Joseph. Your uncle Karl delivered both of my children!"

Before the interview had ended, the fellow stood up and said, "You're hired. Report to the training department on Monday. You'll start as a lineman. Oh, and by the way, you will automatically have two and a half years of seniority going in, due to your service in the navy."

George was feeling a bit blown away. "We hadn't even talked about Ohm's law or anything!" he thought.

He hadn't even needed his fake diploma.

That night, October 6, 1957, one and a half months after his honorable discharge from the US Navy, his father asked him over dinner, "What did you do today, George?"

"Oh, Dad, I went for a job interview. And I got it." Blasé as heck.

Can you imagine the rejoicing, the relief? He reported to work the following Monday.

---

* Roughly 70 percent of the American prison population reads at the third-grade level or below. Many of these are nonreaders like George. It's a supreme challenge to get and keep a good job if you cannot read.

CHAPTER 26

❧

As Spunky's World Turns

AFTER ONLY ONE year of business school, Spunky had acquired all the credits she needed to get her certificate of completion. This worried her, because her father would expect her to come home and work in his restaurant or in a small business in Cottonwood. No! She could not. Now she would take advantage of the opportunity she had with the movie producers at Cudia City. She'd get a taste of the movie business. Would she bite, meet stars and actors, and not look at a hometown boy such as George?

She dressed for the job interview as a professional, of course—she was a graduate of Lamson College—and went to the interview. She was hired. On her first day of work, the predator—oops—producer told her, "You can wear shorts to work here, if you want." *Ding, ding, ding.* Warning bells. The next day, not in shorts, she heard the bells loud and clear: the producer handed her the key to his apartment and told her to go get something from there for him. And that was it. That job was over before it had begun, mercifully. She quit. Her upbringing had imbued her with intuitive thinking and a radar for perps of abuse. Perp-dar?*

Fortunately, the job market was wide open for a trained and certified secretary such as Spunky. To assure that she would not have to go home to Cottonwood, she worked a part-time job at the Valley National Bank until she was offered a plum job—administrative assistant at Phoenix Title and Trust,** a position she would keep for thirty-eight years.

Now her father allowed her to move out of Ramona's home and stay at the downtown Phoenix YWCA. As a career professional in a respectable company, she had the right to determine her living arrangements. She stayed at the Y until she made some work friends and then moved into a shared apartment.

Her single life had now begun.

* Radar for perps.

** The name and ownership changed hands several times over the years. She retired from Transamerica Finance Group.

CHAPTER 27

꘎

Will They Finally Meet?

By 1958, WHEN Spunky was working at the title company and living in the YWCA, George's on-the-job, hands-on-only training with the Mountain Bell Telephone Company was finished, and he had passed it—again, more rejoicing, probably with the consumption of a brew or two with his coworkers. All was well in his world and the country. The general who had saved the world from Hitler was still in the White House. Phoenix was still growing—the postwar growth spurt hadn't ended and never would, it seemed (it still hasn't). Telephones were in nearly every household in America, and telephone lines had to be strung, leaving unattractive poles and lines along roadsides and city streets and avenues running all over town and into the new housing developments. The clean lines of the modern city of Phoenix and the surrounding towns had become cluttered. I blame George.

But oh well. George had a job—a good job! Climbing poles and stringing wire took no reading or detailed writing, other than to mark boxes and sign his name. Now he would be sent out of town to climb poles and tangle up other parts of the state for six years! The worst time on the job was when he worked on the huge poles up in the coldest place in Arizona, between Williams and Flagstaff, when the wind would come down through there and blow hard enough to push him into and hold him onto the one-hundred-foot pole. He could take off his safety gaffe and move around up there unhooked. (Sounds more like unhinged.) He and his crew installed and worked on those poles for eight months, much of the time going up in the morning and staying up all day. They couldn't keep warm with typical Arizona cold-weather gear. George had to borrow a cold-weather army jacket from his brother, who had returned from Vietnam and wouldn't need it anymore.

So what about *them*? What would it take for this couple to get together? Within a year, she had come south and he had gone north—he was there and she was here. It seems they were now on different trajectories, she in his hometown and he in hers. Although there was a five-year difference in their ages, they had started working in their chosen careers at nearly the same time but in different places. Had the stars become misaligned, as far as Spunky and George's potential romance was concerned?

By 1959, George was earning his living by installing the first rotary phones in Prescott, Arizona, and stringing open wire over remote Mingus Mountain, which overlooks Jerome and Cottonwood to the northeast and Prescott down the hill to the southwest. He and his coworkers would need to drive back to roadside motels in Prescott or Cottonwood after a shift; the road going in either direction was winding and narrow and very high in elevation, but that didn't bother Arizona boys. Arizona boys were bred tough and sometimes wild. They didn't mind a bit of danger in their work. And they didn't mind relaxing after a long day of wire stretching. Prescott had Whiskey Row, infamous around the state for a long line of cowboy bars down Gurley Street, across from the courthouse square. George and the fellows would frequent "the Row" when in Prescott, but if they were working out of Jerome (still a ghost town), they would drive down to Cottonwood to eat at the Amigos Inn, the family owned diner with authentic Mexican recipes and good prices.

George, a twenty-seven-year-old man by now, was still single. He didn't want to stay that way forever, but he was not sure how to tell a girl he couldn't read. Well, he hadn't really needed to yet, as he hadn't been serious enough about a girl, at least enough to divulge his secret. Dating was easy enough—dancing or a movie and a casual dinner. He didn't have to read a menu. "What are you going to order?" he'd ask his date. And whatever she said, he'd say, "That sounds good! I'll have the same."

He had learned to love Mexican food over the thirteen years he had been an Arizonan, and there was that great place to eat right there in the center of Cottonwood—the Amigos Inn. Best green chili burritos in the world!

On the weekends, George would drive back to Phoenix with the crew in the company truck, looking forward to some time with his parents and then some nightlife, which hopefully meant he would have a date. Or at least he might meet a lady in a club or a dance hall. He could always find a good dance partner—he loved to dance. George was especially good at the two-step. He was such a good dancer that the girls who wanted to dance with him would often give him what he called the "high sign," a finger wave across the room. He had a shtick—if a girl had not yet given him "the sign," he would first swing dance or two-step with his cousin Lucy, moving in front of a girl he might ask next, so she could see how he danced (peacocked). Then he used his line. Not "Do you want to dance?" but "Do you want to try it?" Clever, George. Anyone will try.

Sarge's Cow Town on South Central Avenue, past the underpass, used to attract young people from all over Phoenix and possibly the entire valley. Country-western was the predominant dance style in most of the dance halls in town and especially at Sarge's Cow Town. Sarge's was in a cavernous, barnlike building and hosted a live country-western band. It had the typical long bar with numerous single guys standing at it, ready to walk onto the dance floor, around which there were tables of attractive, unattached women available for two-stepping, waltzing, and honky-tonk swinging.

Spunky, now twenty-two, and her girlfriends made the rounds on the weekends between Sarge's Cow Town, Siat's Ballroom, and the Riverside Ballroom. Another Phoenician, George Ernst, did the same. By now, George had filled out into a muscular yet lithe man, cute by most young women's standards, and a bit cocky on the dance floor. Spunky was just plain cute, still petite and vivacious.

One night at Sarge's, he noticed her sitting at a round bar table with a group of other girls. She was a "knockout," said George, with long brown hair, and she was just the size he liked. He stood about five foot eight, and she looked to be about five foot three. He made his way across the floor with Lucy to make sure the cute girl in the glasses had seen him. After walking Lucy back to her table, he approached Spunky with "Do you want to try it?" She apparently felt up to the challenge. They danced several times, and during a slow dance, he asked her where she lived.

"I live in Phoenix now, but I'm from Jerome and Flagstaff. I also lived in Cottonwood for a while. I went to business school down here."

"Cottonwood. Oh, sure. I know the area. I work up there, stringing lines over the top of Mingus Mountain. There's a great little Mexican food restaurant up there, I think the best in Arizona. I'm from Phoenix, and I still think it's the best. It's called Amigos Inn."

She leaned back, looked at him slowly, and said, "Yes, I know that restaurant. My parents own it."

The luck of George, saying the right thing at the right time. And he'd never even read the menu!

CHAPTER 28

Dances, Dates, and a Diamond

SHE TOLD HIM her name was Mary Helen, but she had been called Spunky since she was three years old. He could see that the nickname described her personality just right. Alert, fun, independent, not afraid to express herself, and bouncy—that was Spunky then and now. And she was so cute! He couldn't stop looking at her for a long time—she was the darlingest girl he had ever dated. He really, really liked her. She was a lot like George, a person with a strong work ethic instilled during her childhood and her adolescence in the family business. And she was a good Catholic.

The romance proceeded just fine, with one bump in the road that might have been major if Spunky hadn't been so tolerant. George Sr. had not been in Arizona long enough to realize that Mexicans had been here all along and had built Arizona alongside the Anglos. It wasn't that unusual to see mixed couples in Phoenix. One day, a few months into the courtship, George took her by the house to pick up some movie tickets he had left on his dresser. His father was there in a back room, and he decided to walk through the living room, where he saw Spunky sitting, waiting for George. Fuming, he walked to the back of the house and shouted at George, "Get your goddamned Mexican girlfriend out of here!"

The rest of the evening didn't go so well. Somehow, they were able to stay together, even though it was quite awkward between her and his parents as the relationship progressed. But she was not only "spunky"—she was tough and not to be scared off by George

Sr.'s racist mentality. She thought, "His mother and father are such churchgoers, such good Catholics. I don't understand how they could be that way."

She had seen bigotry toward her people in Jerome, where even though the Hispanics and Anglos were friends, worked together, ate together, and played together, they were separated at the public swimming pool and the movie theatre. Mexicans swam only on Thursdays and went to the movies on Wednesdays.

Yet Spunky wanted to be accepted by George's family, so she didn't strike back or make a big deal of the hurtful comment. "I just wanted it to be nice between his parents and me," she explained to me. The tension was hard on Marian, because she, of course, loved her son and wanted Spunky in his life. She was very happy for the young couple. George, however, confronted his father. "Dad, I love Spunky, and if you can't accept her, I'll move out and I won't come back." He was no longer the adolescent who needed his father to get him through life; he was making a good life on his own, and it included Spunky, the girl he loved. Dad seemed to try to be OK with it for a while, but there was always tension.

But I Can

The day George knew he loved her, he decided to buy her a diamond ring. By that time, he had finished the work on Mingus Mountain and was reassigned back in Phoenix, making it convenient for him to see Spunky on a regular basis. He stayed at his parents' house, the house he had grown up in. Why not? He liked to save money, and his father appreciated the financial help.

He decided to show his mother the ring.

"George, I'm so happy for you! You're going to ask Spunky to marry you!"

At that he replied, "Oh no, Mom. I can't ask her to marry me yet. She doesn't even know I can't read."

His mother, looking forward to grandchildren, was chagrined, but more than that, she realized he needed to be honest with Spunky. "George, you have to tell her you can't read. It's only fair."

Because his mother was his guiding light, his guardian angel, he knew she was right. That evening after taking Spunky out to dinner, he drove her up to their favorite parking spot at the top of a hill on McDowell Road, overlooking the city of Phoenix. It was December, and the Phoenix air had a crisp, cold nip in it, just right for cuddling in the car. He turned to her and said, "Spunky, I have good news and bad news. The good news is I love you very much. The bad news is I can't marry you yet, because I can't read or write."

Did George have the absurd hope that he would learn to read over the next few months or years now? Telling her he couldn't read was a bold step into uncertainty. He wasn't sure what her reaction would be—would she ask him to take her home right away? Would she insist he was kidding? She had seen him look at menus plenty of times, which he did to throw people off. But she had wondered. He always ordered the same meal-- green chili burritos--wherever they went. What would she say?

She said only three words. She said, "Well, I can."

She must have really loved him. It wasn't like George was the only guy to care about Spunky. She was popular, cute, fun, and fun loving. And now she would make a commitment that would last more than half a century. And there was that feeling she couldn't help but feel—"I knew that I could help him," she explained when asked why she said yes to his proposal. She would marry George.

They enjoyed a year long engagement after she accepted his proposal that night in the car overlooking the city. All was well in George's world. He had a girl who would overlook his handicap, and she had a ring and a ruggedly handsome, stable man. Compared to the way George's dad had "accepted" her, Spunky's parents merely pointed out to her after she told them of George's handicap, "Well, you know what you are getting into."

Did she?

CHAPTER 29

The Social Event of the Year, Married Life, and a Baby

To CALL THE wedding and reception elaborate would be an understatement. It was, but it also was so much more. The couple set a date, and the church was reserved. They chose the Holy Family Catholic Church in the Jaurequis' hometown of Jerome. Father John Atucha had baptized and confirmed Spunky and performed her first Holy Communion, so of course he would do the honors. He was an institution in the town—he had stayed there with the other diehards when the mine closed—so it would have been a slap in his face to not be chosen. Not only did he perform the wedding ceremony, but between the accolades and the vows, he threw in a bit of a fiery sermon, referring to "all those people at the bar down the street right now, drinking and smoking"—he might have mentioned "hellfire and brimstone." There were so many attendees at this social event of the year that Father Atucha took advantage of the deep pockets from Phoenix and took up a collection. Wedding guests who lived in or were from Jerome wouldn't have batted an eye; Father Atucha was a known entity. However, the guests from Phoenix—George's friends—searched each other out to make eye contact and raise eyebrows. Who gave a sermon like this at a wedding? And who took up a collection?! Meet Father Atucha.

The wedding had it all—sentimentality and cultural tradition, God, admonitions, decorum, beauty all around, and a collection with a sermon. And some family. Spunky's proud parents and all her cousins and their children were there; her sister's son, Bobby Gomes, was her ring bearer. George's parents, however, were *not* there; nor were his siblings, who were too young to travel to Jerome without their parents. George Sr. was still holding himself to his standard of self-righteous prejudice, and holding his wife to his standard. How sad that must have been for Marian. Only George's godfather, Joe Banks, was there to represent the Ernst family. Spunky was an absolutely beautiful and glowing young bride, and her proud bridegroom gazed adoringly at her while she faced the camera, happy and uncomplicated. She looked sixteen but was twenty-two and content with her considered choice. If the wedding pictures forecast the success of this union, the marriage would be fine. He looked twenty-one but by now was twenty-seven. They weren't children; they were both satisfied with their careers and had so much else in common—shared cultural mores and the same marriage-promoting religion. They were "true Americans," the early sixties version, definitely planning to remain married and monogamous for life and looking forward to starting a family. And probably not five people in the audience knew that George couldn't read.

And the reception! Señor Jaurequi had traveled to Hermosillo to hire a renowned mariachi band for this special occasion. Try to imagine the music, the dancing, and the food—catered, of course, by the "best Mexican food restaurant in Arizona," according to George and Spunky. How late did the crowd dance, how much did they eat, and how much tequila and Corona did that crowd consume? I can hear that party in my head even now. George and Spunky slipped out that night and went on their honeymoon in Prescott. They emerged four mornings later and came back to the hotel to find the mariachi band still playing!

"Wow!" he said to his bride. "Your family!"

Married Life

Now Spunky had her handsome mate, whom she would complete, so to speak, and George had a feisty wife with baggage of her own. That's the beauty of good coupling. If it's right, both parties are made better people. George had deep respect for women when he married Spunky, and she had known and dated enough guys around town to realize that George would be there for her where others might not. And we know what she would do for George. The phrase "You complete me" wasn't as commonly used in their young married days, but it would apply most thoroughly to this couple.

The young Ernsts moved into a small duplex apartment at Sixth Avenue and Roosevelt near the downtown area, close to both of their workplaces. They met other young married couples and did what modern young people did for fun—went to movies, played cards at home with friends, and continued dancing at the western ballrooms. On occasional weekends, they would drive the one hundred miles to Cottonwood to see her parents—and of course eat at the Amigos Inn. They even created another couple. George's best friend, Bill Cramer, and Spunky's best friend, Jan, eventually tied the knot themselves, probably just to spend time with the Ernsts. These two couples became a fun foursome.

George and Spunky stayed in their jobs, and she started the great habit of walking to her work at Phoenix Title on West Adams Street, only ten blocks away from their duplex. One morning as she strode briskly toward Central Avenue, a man in a business suit and with a briefcase walked past her in the opposite direction. As he did so, he patted Spunky on the rear end, disarming her completely. She told George about the incident later that evening over dinner, and he was livid, so much so that he called the police. They came to the house and took a report but made it clear that there was nothing they could do about one pat on the butt. "Did you know him?" they asked.

"No, but I know what he looks like!"

George was incensed that they weren't going to do something, and he threatened to take care of it himself. "I'll follow her to work tomorrow, and if she sees him, I'll handle it!"

Later in the week, the Ernsts got a call from the police sergeant who had taken the complaint. "We've had another report. We'd like to ask you to help us catch the guy." They really didn't want George to try to handle it on his own and do something stupid.

So Spunky was enlisted in her own little sting operation. Several plainclothes officers would be in place around the area where she had encountered the perp. If she saw him, she was to give them a sign to indicate his location.

Day one—nothing. Day two—bingo! There he was, coming toward her. She gave the sign, and the officers converged on him, arresting him on the spot.

George flourished in his work. His job was mostly hands-on, and of course he asked Spunky for help with any reading that came up. He was in the prime of his life, and he looked it. In a 1964 photo of him with his line crew, he stands out in the front line, healthy looking and handsome, his chest out like a boxer. He and Spunky were still in the little duplex apartment at Sixth Avenue and Roosevelt. They had only one more aspect of their marriage to fulfill—a child.

Baby Days!

One very special day in the late spring of 1965, Spunky made the announcement most men love to hear. "George, we're going to have a baby."

George was stunned. Did he not know how this had happened? Was he going to respond or just stand there staring at her? The words that came out of his mouth were seemingly unseemly. "What are we gonna do about it?"

Not the response a married woman wants to hear at such a juncture, especially a practicing Catholic. She thought he was implying that she could have an abortion or give the baby away—which is probably not what he meant at all, but he had a hard time clearing up the comment, and Spunky was not amused, nor was she understanding.

"George, we're gonna have a baby and raise the baby!" she responded. She may have sounded calm and collected, but in fact, she was hurt and hormonal and felt aggrieved to the point that she went over to her mother-in-law's house and talked to Marian about George's reaction.

Dear Marian graciously calmed her down, and George did as well—he didn't know why his surprise at the news came out that way, but he's sure he meant something like "Do we paint the spare bedroom in the apartment, where we have our stuff stored?" He definitely wanted that baby!

And on January 16, 1966, a dearly anticipated boy was born in St. Joseph's Hospital to happy and relieved parents. The pregnancy was unremarkable; George remembers only one thing about the labor. "She kept kicking the sheet off her legs, and I kept putting it back on!"

Twelve hours after arriving on the maternity unit, orderlies wheeled Spunky out of the delivery room. She saw George in the hall and called out, "George, you've got your boy!"

In response, George started for the door and called out, "OK, I'll see ya! Gotta go tell the folks!"

And out he ran to drive to his parents' house on Twenty-Fourth Street.

"Pop, Mom—George Ernst III is here! C'mon down and see him. I think I'll call him Trey—get it? Kinda like three in Spanish!"

No idea how George Sr. was handling that, but the natural order is that everyone loves a grandchild, and they change the relationship between the parents and grandparents.

Grandmother Anita Jaurequi came to stay for a few days to help her daughter with her new baby. While there, she burned her hand on the stove and wanted some Noxzema to dress her wound. George took her to the drugstore to buy it. She looked and looked on the shelves for it and couldn't find it. George walked up and pointed to the deep-blue box with the white letters and said, "There it is!"

She looked at him quizzically and said, "I thought you couldn't read!"

Sure, but of course he could recognize the box and the white letters. He had developed strategies and methods to "read" over those many years of illiteracy; he could pass as a reader. Almost everyone in Phoenix used Noxzema for their sunburns, the shimmery white waxlike substance in the blue jar in the blue box. Color coding.

CHAPTER 30

⚬

How She and Others Helped Him

PEOPLE IN GEORGE'S life who didn't know his secret want to know, now that the George Ernst secret is out, "How did Spunky help him?" Compared to the previous women in his life—Marian, the girls at school—Spunky's involvement was times ten. At home, she read the parts of the paper to him that he wanted to hear, based on the headlines that she read aloud first. When he got home from work, she read his mail to him. She probably did the family income taxes.* If he needed to read the directions to setting up a new appliance, there she was. Warnings and precautions on medications? She was there.

But what about work? How did she help him there?

Pretty much the same way many of those other girls and women, starting with the pretty little girl in grade one and then his mother and grandmother, had helped him—covertly. Except now, he and his accomplice communicated by phone.

"Spunky, how do you spell 'customer'? I left the note card in my locker. OK, thanks. See you later. Love you."

He had been getting by for several years by calling family members for help with spelling on his work reports, memorizing key words, and finding the addresses he was assigned to on the city map. After he married Spunky, he of course called her for this type of help, and because he worked for the telephone company, he always had access to a telephone. How propitious. Her office mates at Phoenix Title and Trust probably just thought he was a loving and devoted new husband.

George had the self-confidence he needed to present himself as a fully functioning human being, and he thought his secret was safe from peers and supervisors at work. But it's kinda like the woman who, upon standing up in the public toilet, accidently tucks her skirt into her undies and walks around like that at work or the airport or some other public place without knowing it, exposing herself for at least a few minutes. When someone finally tells her, there is over-whelming embarrassment, until a few minutes later she shrugs her shoulders and thinks, "Oh well, it's just my butt. Everyone has one." She acts as if it didn't happen. But not everyone is a nonreader, and George had hidden it well—or so he thought.

That Day at the Grocery Store

George often helped Spunky with the grocery shopping because she worked full time as well. He could easily shop for cereal and other packaged foods that are easily distinguishable and identifi-able on the shelves. One day he saw his supervisor, Oscar, at the Safeway market with his wife. George, who, as Spunky describes him, "would talk to a dead man," of course struck up a conversation with Oscar and his wife. After a few minutes, George pushed his cart off down the aisle. Oscar, unintentionally within hearing dis-tance of George, whispered, "That's the guy I told you about at work who can't read or write!"

He and his supervisor never spoke of it. It wasn't his butt that was showing; it was the sensitive point of his ego. George contin-ued to perform his duties with Spunky at the end of a phone line.

* Tax preparation used to be user friendly enough for typical citizens to file their own.

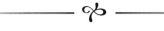

Homeowners at Last

SPUNKY BEGAN TO look around for a home in the older neighborhoods near downtown and found a small ranch-style home in what is known as the Wilshire area, where no house is alike and most are cozy. The Ernsts bought the home on Cambridge Avenue and began to raise their son there and establish lasting relationships with other families. The home had been built in the 1940s, after the war, when the men stationed at Luke Airfield west of Phoenix were deciding to stay in the desert area they had come to love or at least like. Phoenix and its surrounding cities—Tempe, Scottsdale, Avondale, Glendale, Peoria—still had wide-open spaces right in town, mostly covered in dirt and dust and not much else. The sense of freedom and openness in the West made up for the dust and the summer heat. The heat had somehow become a point of pride and created bragging rights with which to impress out-of-town friends and each other. Even though air conditioning had been invented, the more common way to stay cool in a typical Phoenix home was by the use of evaporative coolers, which processed water through straw pads in front of an internal fan. These metal boxes were on the roofs of every home in town. Inside the home, the musty fragrance of wet straw infused the air and created a man-made humidity. Some loved it, and some hated it, but everyone used it—until the early '60s, when air conditioning became affordable. Then installing the "Carrier" on top of the house became a status symbol, and the delightful, soggy swamp coolers started disappearing.

What would happen to George if his job became obsolete or technology upgraded the system and he had to pass a test or read information every day to complete his job? How did he live with that sword of Damocles hanging over him? If his secret came out and they canned him, what then?

Insurance. They bought insurance in the form of a rental property. George had learned good money-management skills from his father. Together, he and Spunky had saved enough money to invest. They purchased a little two-bedroom home on North Eighteenth Street, with a separate guesthouse in the back for a single person. George now had a backup plan as a landlord. It was close enough to their home that George could go and collect the rent in person and do the simple repair jobs often necessary on rental homes. One time, when he picked up the rent from a family of three—mom, dad, and teenage daughter—he got quite a surprise.

"Yoo-hoo. It's George. It's the first of the month. Can I come in?"

"Come on in, George. We're at the dinner table."

In he came, and there they were at the dinner table, eating—*au naturel.* That's right—nude.

"Oh, excuse me! I can come back later!" He tried to look away.

"No, no! It's fine. The check's on the table in the living room. George…have you ever heard of Shangri La?* It's out by the air force base…come join us sometime!"

"Sure, yeah…I'll look into it! Have a great day! Thanks for the check!"

The shock of it cut short his usually garrulous nature that day.

In the same vein, one morning he called the single woman living in the guesthouse in the back of the property to ask if he could pick up the check while she was at work.

"Sure, George. It'll be in the medicine cabinet in the bathroom."

"Hmmm. Why?" he wondered. "A strange place to hide a check."

But there it was, with an added bonus—a Polaroid photo of the renter herself *au naturel*. First, the nudists—that was innocent. They do that. But the naked lady in the medicine cabinet? That's just obviously a come-on! That scrawny kid his Uncle Karl had delivered and the 120-pound little banty rooster who barely graduated from grade eight had grown into a good-looking man. If not quite handsome, he was definitely what women would call "cute." Although not a real cowboy, he was what Glen Campbell called a "rhinestone cowboy," with the boots and fancy belt buckle and usually a big ring. He wore the Levi jeans as well as the next guy and had maintained a toned body by climbing telephone poles on a daily basis. That's how men kept their physiques before the advent of body-building gyms on every corner—they worked hard.

A very serious and sad occurrence happened to George the landlord at a later date and with a different renter. By now, Frank, George's brother, was living in the front house of the property. He had returned from Vietnam and was probably a victim of PTSD. Another veteran was renting the guesthouse in the back. One day, Frank called George. "George, you gotta come over here and check out the place. There's a really bad smell coming from the little house."

That's right. The guy had pulled the trigger. Surely this type of event is the worst experience a landlord can have. George cleaned up the mess and made it presentable for a new renter.

* Shangri La was a clothing-optional resort area.

CHAPTER 32

— ❧ —

Good-Bye, Mom and Dads

THE ERNSTS FELT the impact of losing three of their four parents in the mid to late '70s. Spunky's father succumbed at age sixty-six to liver cancer in August 1976. He was buried in the Cottonwood cemetery, near to his beloved family restaurant.

As awful and painful as Roberto Jaurequi's lingering demise was, George Ernst Sr. intended his death to be quick and painless, a way to end the emotional pain he was going through. He chose to go fast and in his own time, causing the near-end of his previously happy-seeming life by his own hand. His emotional pain was caused by the loss of his much-loved wife.

His beautiful, devoted, and happy life partner, Marian, had passed away the previous year while vacationing in Long Beach, California, where she and George Sr. spent many of their summers in a cabin on the pier near their married children and their spouses. Breast cancer killed her because she never sought the diagnosis she needed when symptoms first occurred and then persisted.

Ironically, it took her husband's stay in the hospital for Marian to get the information she feared. While there for a goiter treatment, George Sr. implored his doctor, "Please take a look at my wife's breast. She won't go to the doctor for it, but she has a lump—a big one."

So the doctor did, and he was quite concerned and insisted on an X-ray immediately. The "lump" had grown all the way into her back muscles and had adhered to her spine. It wasn't long before she was terminal; in fact, she died soon after on their planned vacation in Long Beach. Her children had been called from Phoenix to gather round her, and soon, they were planning a funeral. Much changed for George Sr. His beautiful wife was gone. Within weeks, his daughter, Mary Ernst, George's younger sister, got married and left home. Dad grew extremely despondent after losing Marian, and now his daughter was out of the house. He didn't do loneliness well. He had depended on his wife more than anyone realized. George Jr. realized this after his father's death and told Spunky, "Let's not get that close!" And he started insisting they take vacations and other activities apart from each other.

Why would Marian not seek a doctor's advice about the lump in her breast? The answer was denial and fear.

When the Ernst family went to Long Beach to say their final good-byes and to bring Marian's body back home to Phoenix, Spunky had stayed in Phoenix for work while George handled arrangements to get the casket home and buried in St. Francis Cemetery. Spunky was tasked to be at Sky Harbor Airport to meet the casket and Mr. Ernst, who escorted it. After she and George Sr. had delivered the body to the funeral home, she drove him to his home and walked him to his door and asked if he needed anything, saying, "Could I help in any way?"

"No, thank you," he replied. He closed the back door where she had dropped him. She walked around the corner of the house and past the kitchen window. She caught a glimpse of him standing there, where he had stepped over to look out the window at her. With a short hand wave, she walked past the next set of windows in the dining area next to the kitchen—and there he was again! She stopped and asked through the window, "What can I do for you, Mr. Ernst?"

He tried at first to avert his eyes, but he had a task he knew he needed to complete. He looked at her and said, "I...need to apologize for all the times I was unpleasant to you over the years."

Her first reaction—which fortunately she kept to herself—was "It's about time. You're a few years late."

If she had said that aloud, how differently his amends would have ended. But she held her tongue and remained clear of conscience.

This was 1976. Marian and George Ernst had shared a forty-four-year life together, and he had depended on her for so much—companionship, food, and emotional support. His sadness at her death could not be lifted. Now he felt alone and adrift. He couldn't get his sense of equilibrium back and floundered with his emotions. He kept company with a female friend of both his and Marian's but worried that his children would not approve. He was unable to regain a sense of purpose or serenity. He was bereft.

And so, after a year of agonizing, he shot himself. He lay down on the bed, put a pillow over his head to control the mess, and shot himself. But not successfully, because it didn't kill him. George found him there and called the police department immediately. They realized he was brain-dead but breathing, so they took him to St. Luke's Hospital. That choice was made even though another hospital was closer, because of Catholicism.

The investigating detective on the case, Wally Sims, was an acquaintance of George Jr.'s, and so they spent some time process-ing this horrific event, probably at a bar over a few beers.

"George, there's nothing you could have done. Get that out of your head. He was dead when we picked him up. But the law… he was breathing so we had to take him to the hospital. You say you don't know what to do, so I'll tell you. It sounds terrible, but you have to make a hard decision. You need to be the one to end it for him, because you're the oldest child. You need to pull the plug."

George loved his father so. The man who shepherded him through his adolescence was unresponsive and near death, and George would have to be the one to end it for good. He was Catholic, but he knew it was what was best for his dad. He didn't need to read to perform that heartbreaking task.

CHAPTER 33

Work and Drink like a Man

GEORGE WAS A guy who enjoyed doing guy stuff, like climbing poles with a sturdy leather cable gaffe secured around his haunches, like making money on the side with rentals or schemes of usury in the navy, like dancing the half-step with women whose hair swung and smelled like peaches and lavender, and like drinking till his head felt light and he swaggered across a barroom floor to get to the men's room—where he could get into a true and unspoken pissing contest with the guy standing next to him—guy stuff. All his friends drank, he thought, especially his workmates, so he felt like he was just one of the guys, like any normal person.

"All my friends drank—important people, bankers, politicians. We called ourselves the Seventh Avenue Boys Club. We drank at all the bars along Seventh Avenue from Roosevelt to Camelback Road. The Chez Nous, Emerald Room, Blue Grotto, Green Frog, Side Door."

Most charitable organizations start out with a cause, and then the participants go out drinking together. The Seventh Avenue Boys Club started as a drinking gang and then, to legitimize it, established a charity around itself.

"We had two charity events a year—a Christmas party and a golf tournament. One year, we decided to order Seventh Avenue Boys Club T-shirts, so we ordered two hundred XL T-shirts.

"The T-shirt proprietor called and asked our fellow who had placed the order, Charlie Williams, 'Are you sure you guys want that many XL T-shirts? Do you have that many boys that big?"

Charlie explained the nature of the "boys" club, and hearing that disclosure, the shop owner guffawed. "You guys are gettin' a ten percent discount."

At work, George performed his duties with expertise and kept his employer and customers satisfied. He earned cost-of-living raises and never received a bad review; in fact, his job reviews always ranked him either at the highest level or right below that, and over the years, he received several certificates of recognition.

"George," his supervisor hollered across the room. "Look here. Your schmoozing has paid off again. You got a special certificate from the girls in the dispatch office, for 'Sunshine Disposition and Cooperation.' You can put that one with the one you received that time for 'Recognition of Excellent Service' from one of your favorite customers."

On October 9, 1982, George completed twenty-five years of service to Mountain Bell. He had advanced over the years from line-man to cable splicer and then to repairman, everybody's hero. His social nature was pleased that he was able to meet some of the customers he helped, as he would go to the front door and tell them that he would be working on the line back there.

"They'd come out and talk to you. I had a lady once over at Twelfth Street and Van Buren who would bring me a piece of lemon meringue pie when I worked on her line. She had a lot of trouble. Sometimes a hard rain would knock out certain area phones every time."

Yeah, yeah, a pretty girl, George. They always gravitated to you, didn't they!

Frequent repairs would be done to boxes on the trunk lines on busy roads like Baseline Road, which several decades ago were on the far outskirts of town. Baseline runs between Tempe and Phoenix, and in those days, it attracted gawkers looking at the beautiful Japanese flower gardens, which stretched from fragrant and beautiful mile to the next fragrant and beautiful mile. At night, it was a good way to get back from Tempe or vice versa and avoid the city squad cars. Either way, drivers ran into those poles with regularity, and guys like George would need to repair them. In town, zealous pigeon haters would shoot at the birds while they sat on the telephone lines and often miss the pigeons. Boom—cable out. It needed to be repaired. George and his coworkers had plenty of work.

He continued to meet the phone company's work and customer--service standards and often surpassed them, even while maintaining his after-hours activities with his "charity." He not only did a good job but still looked good doing it, hanging there off the pole in the jeans he filled out well and the snug T-shirt exposing his defined chest and biceps. His lifelong fastidiousness about his appearance had paid off with a fit body even in his late forties.

As far as he knew, only one guy—a partner he couldn't keep it from, Don H.—knew about his reading problem. Spunky could help him study the safety manuals, but someone had to cover for him on the job occasionally. On at least one occasion, Don became his partner in crime like Bill had been when he filled out the navy application for George.

One day, George came home from work and appeared to be agitated about something. Spunky asked him, "What's wrong, George?"

He admitted, "They're giving the test next week. I have to study these manuals. I don't know how I'm gonna take it. I can't bring it home."

"Who else is taking it?"

"All the guys; you know, Bob and Mike and Don."

"OK. Don's taking it? Is he taking it the same day as you are scheduled?"

"I don't know."

"Don knows your problem. Ask him to pick up two answer sheets and make a copy of his test when he finishes it and give it to you. You bring home both sheets, the blank one and the one with his answers, and you'll fill out your sheet here, using his. I'll read the questions and his answers to you so you can make sure you would pass the test if you had to do it yourself. Make sure you schedule your test for the next day!"

Amazingly, this test heist was pulled off. The day George was scheduled to take the test, he wore a large work shirt—neatly pressed, as usual—and when it came time to take the test, he surreptitiously pulled out the completed test from under his shirt and turned it in.

George had probably been practicing variations of sleight of hand his entire life, at school and work. Once again he had to rely on subterfuge to accomplish what had to be done. How long could he keep up the pressure?

OK, it's not like this test was the ACT or SAT, and obviously it was not a seriously considered mark of competence, or there would have been better test security around it. George's work was always performance based, and he was known for his good to excellent performance on the job. But the stress of covering up his disability for so many years, making sure he didn't make mistakes, and always living up to the highest expectations of the company had to be a factor in his need to take a few drinks at the end of a shift, whether he knew it or not.

George wasn't finished at twenty-five years. He'd go for the full forty-years retirement package. In 1990, he went from the heights of a thirty-five-foot telephone pole to the depths of an underground tunnel when he accepted a lateral transfer to the new Deep-Underground Air Maintenance group, checking the air pressure on cables in manholes. But first, he had to complete the "cable-pressurization theory and practice" course. Who knows how? We know how. Spunky. She went through the manuals with him at night after dinner, just like his father had done with him when he worked as an electrician's apprentice forty years earlier.

The cable-pressurization exam may have been the test that Don helped him with. For legal purposes, we'll just keep the exact date and job description the test was designed for undeclared. We don't want to hear about old retired Mountain Bell executives tearing their hair out and passing out on the golf course. Besides, who could argue with those positive performance reviews? His final performance review for his underground work was evidence when his supervisor wrote that "George meets and sometimes exceeds standards as a Network Facilities Technician." He could always read numbers and gauges, and he could memorize the look of the few necessary words he had to recognize. He's a fortunate man that he retired before everything had to be input into a computer. It might have made his work more complicated. And fortunately, all the training for the positions he took were apprenticeships on the job.

Underground repair work entailed dropping down into a three-by-four-foot manhole, replacing old cable, and splicing and attaching new cable, using tone, color coding, and numbers—George's forte. The city had started burying the lines in 1966, at least in newer neighborhoods, and citizens were fascinated by the work going on underground in front of their homes and workplaces. There was a manhole every 350 feet, to accommodate the linemen.

"When I worked on the cable in front of St. Mary's School, a certain priest would come out and watch me work. I was down in that box for three months. Got to know him pretty well," George recounted.

In 1994, his appraisal was a repeat of the previous one: "Meets all standards, is never absent and never tardy." And yes—he was still drinking, which he often did the night before the scheduled safety meetings.

"Once a month when I was working underground, we had a safety meeting. We would pass the safety manual around and read out of it. When it was my turn to read I always had a reason to pass:

'Not feeling good,' 'Was welding last night and got something in my eye,' (for that excuse I would wipe some Vaseline under my eyes for visual effect), or 'Forgot my reading glasses.'"

If he had just said something to his employers, would they not have made accommodations for him, by the mid-1990s at least, and probably before? In 1990, the comprehensive Americans with Disabilities Act* had been passed by Congress, and employees now had protection against discrimination at work. But the secret was so ingrained into his personality and his psyche now that it didn't occur to him to bring it up.

What was it like for George to work from the heights of a telephone pole to under the streets of Phoenix?

"All you're concerned about is the work. You don't think about being "up there" or "down there." You just concentrate on stringing those lines, repairing the lines, replacing the cable. It's just a place. Freezing cold or hot as hell—it's just a place."

And then, 1996—his retirement ceremony. What an amazing accomplishment.

"George, here is your watch—it just happens to be a grandfather clock, so that you will have something to do every evening. Remember us as you wind it! Use this Rolex to check the time by." George didn't mention it, but he could have bought his own Rolex. He had retired with a million dollars in his profit-sharing account.

And as he likes to say, "It's all about the color coding!" Yeah. Green.

* https://en.wikipedia.org/wiki/Americans_with_Disabilities_Act_of_1990

CHAPTER 34

Spunky's Bad News

THE FIRST TIME I met Spunky, she was wearing the pink Susan G. Komen T-shirt, the one worn by the runners in the annual 10K breast-cancer awareness race in Phoenix, Arizona. I said, "Oh, I see you are wearing the shirt. Do you run the race?"

"No, I don't run it—I'm a survivor! Double mastectomy!" And with that she pulled the shirt out from her chest with her thumbs and fingers to suggest boobs. I knew then how she had acquired her nickname. Feisty, open, energetic—her mom pegged her at three years old.

She never lost the nickname because she stayed that way. The insistent child had evolved into a woman who knew what she wanted and pursued it. That didn't mean she was rebellious or did things "her way" only. No, she had always been able to balance societal norms and her will with ease. And unlike her mother-in-law, she paid attention to medical developments and took medical advice. Self-breast examination to detect dimples or lumps in a breast was advice she took.

One morning in 1991, she made the discovery that can make a woman's knees go weak and spread a chill throughout her body even while standing in a warm shower.

"George, I might have found a lump."

And unlike George's mother, who probably never checked and hadn't even reported an abnormality in the breast and therefore died with it, Spunky wasted no time getting a doctor's appointment. Within five days of her diagnosis, she was in surgery. She insisted on a full mastectomy to remove the tumor right away and started preparing for the possibility that she might die. She cleaned out her closets and gave away a cherished emerald ring to her best friend. She began her six-week course of chemotherapy and continued her life as previously conducted, developing new friendships along the way with fellow patients at the chemo center and through a breast-cancer support group, the Bosom Buddies.

She continued to work at the title company, using her accumulated sick leave for the hospital stay and chemo days. She walked a mile to and from her chemo treatments and kept her house up as ever. The whirlwind existence can be attributed to her Spunkiness, her energy level, and her faith. She didn't stop her regular activities. Having held the informal title of Watchdog of Cambridge Avenue for the past several years, she continued in that role and walked the street regularly, watching for suspicious behavior or things out of place.

Her devotion to and support of George throughout the years was reciprocated by him during her cancer scare and treatment. He was afraid for her, of course, but he remained in awe of her fortitude and businesslike approach to her condition and fierce approach to her survival.

"Her faith in God and in her doctors gave me the inspiration to give all my support and love to her, and it paid off," he told me.

"He'd run to get me a taco if I mentioned that's what I wanted. He learned quickly that I might not want one in an hour and might be too nauseated to eat it. So he'd just go," Spunky added.

"To see her in such a vulnerable condition, it frightened me but awed me, too. I loved her even more than before to watch her go through that."

One week after her final chemo treatment, she went to her high school reunion with her head in a scarf. She pretty much had to go—as usual, she had helped organize it. And it wouldn't have been the same without Spunky Jaurequi!

A few months later, Spunky opted for breast reduction in her left breast to even things out. During that process, cancerous cells were discovered. After she awoke in the recovery room, the doc told her. Without a second thought, she said, "Doc, let's get this sucker off!" On St. Patrick's Day, 1993, she had her second breast removed. She has been cancer-free since. The cancer probably doesn't dare come back.

Spunky not only joined Bosom Buddies but held many of the meetings in her home. George had a typical dopey, chauvinistic response the first time he saw those ten or twelve women sitting in his living room. "There's all those gals here and not a single chi chi."

He must have thought that all breast-cancer survivors had experienced doubles, as had Spunky.

It was a time when men either fall apart or man up, and George cut down on his male-bonding boozing. But that wouldn't last.

CHAPTER 35

— ✂ —

Semi-Independent Lives

WHEN HIS FATHER had fallen into despondency and committed suicide a year after Marian's death, George had made the emotional decision that he and Spunky shouldn't become as dependent on each other as his parents had been, perhaps out of fear for his own mental health if she were to die before him. It was more probable that he would fall apart than would she. So being a man's man, and in the spirit of "Let's not get that close" (which, of course, they already were), George actively began to participate in fishing excursions to Mexico, where the drinking was excusable. Starting in the late 1980s, he and a bunch of buddies started going to Ensenada for a couple of weeks every summer over a period of a few years, forming lifelong friendships and reveling in the camaraderie of male bonding. But remember—he had always had a pretty little girl by his side to help him get by, and yes, he met a pretty girl the first time he went to Ensenada. And of course she helped him, but *not like that!* He met this young Mexican woman—a teenager, actually—while he was out on a shopping excursion. Elizabeth was selling decorative household tile in a little shop, and George, who would "talk to a dead man" or in this case to a sweet young salesgirl making a living behind a counter in Mexico, was just doing his thing—talking. Maybe bragging. It was, after all, a fishing trip. And George is bilingual, so he could have bragged in Spanish! Before the trip was over, Elizabeth, her boyfriend, and her mother had practically adopted him. They shared home-cooked meals with him, and of course she tried to sell him some tile. Every ensuing trip to Ensenada included a visit to Elizabeth and her family. There was nothing physical or unseemly about the friendship; she was young enough to be his daughter. In a way, they just adopted each other. Over the years, he has spent time with her mother, her husband, and her children, and eventually, there will be grandchildren. The relationship can probably be explained by George's innate love for family. He has always been in a healthy family, and that is the source of his well-being and security. So in an effort to not get so close to his wife that it would kill him, he adopted another family in another country. He proudly shows the pictures of her and her children in his Mexico photo album. Spunky is fully aware of Elizabeth and her family and has spoken to her over the phone. Spunky just says, "Oh well."

While George was cavorting in Mexico, Spunky considered his proposition to "not get that close" and thought, "OK!" Tessie (her sister) and Rosie (her friend) lived in town and were game to play. So that's what she did.

The women started going to the casinos that ring the outskirts of Phoenix for the slot machines and the concerts. Sometimes they traveled to Las Vegas and Laughlin, each a quick plane ride or a six-hour drive from Phoenix. The low lights, the party atmosphere, and the casinos provided an enjoyable diversion for her. Seeing people other than her secretarial colleagues and the buttoned-down executives at the title company was energizing and interesting. George had no interest in gambling, so their separate vacations made sense to both of them. They maintained a peaceful coexistence characterized on occasion by different diversions.

But one time, George drew the line.

Spunky's sister Tessie called her with the news, "Sis, Julio Iglesias is in concert in Vegas next month. Start planning."

Spunky planned and then told George of her plans. George said, "Sure, you can go. But I'm going with you!"

The women allowed their husbands to tag along, knowing it meant more spending money for themselves.

Julio Iglesias was the sexiest, handsomest, sweetest male Spanish vocalist to ever make it big in the United States. He was an international star. Women swooned. Men shook their heads but admitted his talent. Even young girls found the middle-aged crooner irresistible. Of course the couples would go see him in Vegas. He was a Latino, he sang in the ladies' language, and they and millions of other women around the world just loved him. If you didn't and you were a woman, you might want to check your pulse. The night of the concert, Spunky and Tessie left the guys in the rooms to dress and went down to wait around the lobby to see if they could get an early glance at Julio. As they left the elevator, they could see a crowd converging in the hallway across the lobby. Having an instinct for action, Spunky dragged her sister over there and got behind some people. Someone whispered, "They say he's coming through the kitchen now!"

Spunky's short but fearless. She could easily slip through this crowd and didn't hesitate to do so. She called back to her sister, "He's in the hall!"

Tessie called out, "Well, run up to him and kiss him! I dare you!"

He was nearly on top of her, maybe six feet away. She froze but not for long. Her instincts kicked in, and without thinking, she simply walked up to him and stood on her tippy-toes, and well, what would you do? She kissed him. Quickly, of course. She didn't want to end up on the front page of the *National Enquirer*. But it was enough. He was mildly flustered but obviously used to such treatment; he thanked her. She thanked him. And no concert ever meant as much to her after that!

One year later, she and her niece went to Graceland, the mecca for ladies who love Elvis. George didn't go. He probably went fishing.

Spunky had another reason to look forward to being out of the house on weekends. George's drinking was creating resentment for her. "Here I've had to read to him for all these years, and now I have to put up with *this*?" she told me. What had been just getting a beer after work with the guys once in a while was becoming habitual. He had become a regular at the American Legion, the traditional fraternal watering hole for servicemen no longer in service. That's when he wasn't spending time with his drinking club. He had been able to slow down the drinking with his friends during her cancer experience, but with her in good health and her old independent self again, he resumed at the same level. Over a period of five or six years after the cancer, it got really bad—he drank mostly on weekends, but one or two evenings during the week he'd come home drunk and late, after she had fixed a meal. Thus came the ultimatum.

"George, if you don't stop the drinking, I'm going to divorce you. I can't take it any longer. The drunken behavior, the smell, the lost weekends." Most women married to alcoholics say that at least once, and usually several times over several years. One would think that a man married to a woman like Spunky would have quit right then. Spunky is, after all, spunky—one would think he would take her at her word. Of course he was concerned about her threat, but—as is the case with some men—he didn't know what she was talking about. He thought that if the lawn was mowed and the paychecks were coming in, he was doing his part. (Sorry, George. This is the modern era.)

He had been able to do a complete cover up and run around his illiteracy for nearly his entire long life, so he might have thought, "Nobody else knows," or "All the guys drink like I do." Or before he retired, "It's not a problem at work." And after he retired, "Hey, I'm retired. My time is my own."

Of course all the guys drank like he did—they had established a club with a name proclaiming what the core activity was: the Seventh Avenue Boys Club.

And as is the case with people who really don't want to stop drinking and don't see it as a problem, George still had some drinking to do. It would take an incident.

CHAPTER 36

—— ❧ ——

The Incident Was an Accident

THE YEAR WAS 1998, and the date was December 19. George was sixty-three years old, retired, with too much time on his hands. Spunky had lived through two experiences with breast cancer. She had read to him for thirty-seven years and had provided cover for him at work. She really didn't feel like living with a drunk—illiterate or literate. She had given him the ultimatum, and that hadn't worked. What now? What would it take?

That evening he had been bonding and drinking with his Seventh Avenue Boys Club friends at an establishment close to home called the Side Door. He left drunk close to closing time. Driving home on Seventh Avenue, slowly, of course, as drunks often do, he turned onto his street—West Cambridge—in front of two cars full of teen-agers. One of the cars hit him. Amazingly, the kids weren't hurt, and George merely had minor injuries, providing evidence to the ·old saying that God protects drunks and children. The Ernsts lived a block and a half down from Seventh Avenue, but the impact was so loud that George and Spunky's next-door neighbors, Marianne and Marty, woke up as they heard the crash from their house. They came over and hollered at Spunky through the door, "Let's go down and see what happened."

Spunky had awakened too and replied, "I know who it is. It's George." She was right.

He wasn't badly hurt and didn't go to jail—at least not then—but he did spend the night in the ER. When he got home the next morn-ing, there were three traffic tickets on the dining-room table. He knew what that meant—it meant he would be murdered or divorced by Spunky, or worse, he would be left in the silent treatment to stew in his own juices. And obviously he would have to go to court. At that moment, something happened. He stood there in the dining room, fear and apprehension coursing through his veins, and sincerely asked God to help him quit drinking. He knew he couldn't stop on his own. And from that point on, everything started falling into place. His neighbor Marianne found him an attorney for $2,500. Later that week, he had a hearing at the Motor Vehicle Department. The judge asked the prosecuting attorney, "What's the charges?"

"Severe DUI, your honor."

The judge asked the police officer who had written up the wreck, "Where's the paperwork, Officer?"

"I don't have it, your honor." One charge dropped. Then his attorney did some fancy footwork, and George's driver's license was restored. George's luck strikes again. George believes that in this case it was God—his luck had run out.

But there was still one count against him, and for that he would have to spend a weekend in Sheriff Joe Arpaio's tent. Which he turned into fun. Let's hear your version of "fun" in the tents, George.

"First, the not-so-fun part. There's the holding tank before you even get to the tent. I spent six hours in there with a guy dying from cancer. They had to keep taking him out to give him cancer medication. I finally just asked, 'Why don't you just release him?' That part wasn't fun.

"But then, in the tents, there are two sections—a short-term section for a few days' sentence and a long-term section where guys could go out and work during the day and come back. I was in the short-term for three days. I'd been told I could take some cash in, so I took twenty dollars in quarters and came out with forty dollars. I sold my quarters for one hundred percent interest. That was fun.

"My job that weekend was to get the food to the long-term tent. I'd walk to the kitchen with a deputy. At lunch on Saturday, my first shift, the deputy said, 'Take twelve trays over there to the women's tent.'

"I pushed the cart over to the women's tent. One big gal came up to me and said, 'Give me an extra milk.'

"I said, 'I can't do that; everyone only gets one milk,' because the deputy was right behind me!

"The gal said, 'Give me another milk, and I'll give you a blow job.' So I turned around and said to the deputy, 'She wants to see you when you get off.'

"One night we watched a hockey game on TV. The next night, I went to an Alcoholics Anonymous meeting that some guys brought in from outside. It was raining. The tent didn't leak too bad.

"I've been going to AA meetings ever since."

CHAPTER 37

George Speaks at an AA Meeting

"Hi, I'm George, and I'm an alcoholic.

"First, let me tell you that I don't blame anybody or anything for my alcoholism. I know, people have told me, 'Well, George, it's no wonder you drank like that—not being able to read or write. That must have been hard on you.'

"And to that I have to say, 'No, it's not that.' You see, I never let the reading issue get me down. I was a happy kid. I had a great family. I was loved. Nothing made me drink. I just loved to drink! And don't forget—I'm Irish."

There was laughter from the crowd as he warmed up. He went on.

"When I was a youngster, my cousins and I always snuck some wine at Thanksgiving. That was just expected. But no, if it's what you're thinking, I never drank any of those little whiskey bottles my dad stored under my bed when he was a salesperson for Schenley Whiskey. I couldn't get ahold of them—they served as my box springs!

"But look—I've been in jail at least once in every state I've ever been in! Including Tijuana, Mexico. Any of you Arizona guys will get that."

Knowing chuckles were heard.

"When I was seventeen, I went to Tijuana with some friends for the weekend. I must have done some serious drinking, because on Sunday morning, I woke up in jail with horrible diarrhea, with just my underwear on. They gave me my pants so I could join the crowd in the courtyard, where they were serving beans out of a big vat. Around the courtyard there was an eight-foot fence. I thought, 'I can get over that wall,' but as I looked closer, I could see sitting next to the fence was a big hombre with a Gatling-like gun with the string of bullets. I decided to just call my friends to come get me and help me buy my way out of the jail. I had lost my jacket and diamond ring to those jail "officials," but they wanted more money.

"So I told my buddies, 'Thanks for picking me up; thanks for the loan to get me out. I want to buy your lunch in Tucson.' So we stopped to eat, and when we had eaten our lunch, I said, 'Do you want some pie to go with that?' So they ordered pie, and when the waitress brought it, I said, 'Boys, you'll have to take the pie with you. Let's go.' Dine and dash. I'm not proud of that.

"When I was nineteen, I got myself and my best friend into the navy."

George proudly demonstrated his subterfuge with his feet and explained how Bill Cramer had filled out his forms and later had given him the answers on tests during boot camp.

"I was stationed in Long Beach, California—that was seventh heaven. One night on shore leave, I went into a bar in the town next to Long Beach, San Pedro, and consequently went to jail. The shore patrol got me out. I had to talk to the captain when I got back on the ship. Captain asked, 'What happened?'

"My response was 'They're against me.' I really thought so.

"I had a slush fund to loan money to guys on ship. I loaned five dollars for eight dollars and twenty dollars for thirty dollars. That's how I got my drinkin' money.

"So I was based in Hawaii for a while. We had a ship party, meaning everyone on our shift went over to a bar in town. I was driving my '42 Chevy. The brakes went out, or so I said. I hit a Chinaman and went to prison. (Hawaii wasn't a state yet, so they didn't have city jails.) In there, they de-liced me—shaved my head. My slush-fund partner got me out.

"When I got back stateside after I was discharged, I got a letter postmarked Hawaii. The Chinaman was suing me for one hundred and fifty thousand dollars.

"My attorney told me they couldn't do anything to me from Hawaii but to stay out of Hawaii. Which I did for about sixty years. I think I'm safe now.

"I kept drinking throughout my job. It never kept me from going in to work. I climbed poles for a living, and I never fell off! I was a functional alcoholic right up to the end.

"My drinking at the end of a shift got to the point where it wasn't fun anymore. My wife finally asked me to quit. I thought if I did everything I was supposed to do in the marriage, such as bring home a paycheck and do the yard work, I could drink.

"Then came the wreck. I could have killed those boys.

"And that's when my recovery started, although I didn't know it at the time. The morning after the wreck, I stood in the kitchen, and I actually prayed, not a Catholic prayer but an alcoholic's prayer—God, I need help.

"You probably suspect that because of the wreck, I was given the privilege of spending some time in Sheriff Joe's tent. I think it made a difference. After that, I got into treatment and started going to meetings. And let's just admit it: if you've been in Sheriff Joe's tent, you're likely gonna wind up here in. A.A. someday!"

His recollections continued.

"After spending some not-so-bad time in the tent for three days, I was 'sentenced' to some City of Phoenix drug and alcohol treatment program. They gave us a packet of papers to fill out about our drinking. How was I to fill that out? I got humble for the first time and asked a firefighter who was in there for cocaine abuse to help me out. Yes, of course it was a woman. She sat there next to me, and we filled out our papers together.

"The counselor interviewing me for the city program kept asking me, 'Why do you drink?'

"I told her, 'I'm Irish. You could put the Irishmen who don't drink in a phone booth.'

"And again she asked, so I said, 'My friends drink.' And again, 'Because it was fun.' Again—she was relentless—'Because I can't read or write?'

"'Sure, because, "poor you"?' She persisted.

"Finally, I got angry with the questions, and I responded, 'Because I'm an alcoholic!' And that was my breakthrough. I was already attending AA meetings. I knew then that the meetings would save my life. Now I take meetings into the tents with a group of sober guys. I can tell them I've been there.

"I also can tell everyone I talk to in AA about my illiteracy. It's usually the first thing that comes out of my mouth. It's a good feeling to not have to hide it, to not have to live a lie, at least in these rooms.

"Today I celebrate nineteen years of sobriety. So everyone, join me for a piece of cake and coffee, and thanks for listening. Oh, and I'll read that birthday card you all signed in my next life."

The room erupted in applause, and George made his way through the crowd. As he made his way to the coffee line, a fellow about his age, maybe ten years younger, stopped him. "George, you're the first guy I've ever heard who has told my story, about the reading and writing. I thought I was the only one! But man, I've done time. Hard time. I could never get a good job, and if I did, I couldn't keep it. George, the jails and prisons are full of guys who are illiterate—guys who didn't have the same self-esteem that you did; it was dug right out of 'em by the school system and by ignorant friends and family, telling them they could if they just tried. I'm one of those guys. I'm a functional illiterate. I can read and write about the third-grade level. How about you?"

"I wouldn't know, but I couldn't read my son's first-grade books. I remember that much."

CHAPTER 38

꙳

George Goes to College

AFTER HE GAINED his sobriety, George decided to take some courses at Phoenix College. Perhaps he was hoping that with sobriety, he could learn to read and write. He signed up for Speech 101 and Algebra 1. For his first speech, he used what he knew—a handout called "Twenty Questions." Twenty Questions is the test used by alcohol counselors to help drunks see the extent of their drinking. It asks questions such as "Do you ever take a drink in the morning?" and "Have you lost a friendship or relationship as a result of your drinking?" If even just a few of them are answered yes, it sets off alarm bells. After the class took the test, he basically gave an AA pitch. It was a hit. His teacher thought he was brilliant—the use of the handout, the personalized story—it was brilliant of George to think of it, because the audience had to grade their own tests, and he didn't have to read or write a thing to prepare or deliver his speech. His ingenuity learned out of desperation was still intact.

His second speech was also personal and also about something he knew—from the example of his parents and later from the "marriage encounter" class he took at the Catholic church before his wedding. The topic was "How to keep a marriage." The main point was "The wife is number one." He spoke from the heart and gave lots of examples.

His teacher's response to his speeches?

"George, I never had a student like you before." He got a 96 percent for the course. Finally, academic success.

Algebra was a different story. "I didn't have a problem with arithmetic. I could always add and subtract. Well, multiplication gave me a little trouble, but no one ever told me I had a problem with math."

George found out that addition and subtraction would not be enough to master algebra.

The next year he took only one course—golf. Still, he was going to college!

CHAPTER 39

—— ❧ ——

Life in Retirement

GEORGE IS NOT sitting around reading the paper (oops) and tearing his hair out or railing at the radio talk shows or TV news. Straight out of the chute, he started new activities and continued with his ongoing fishing trips to Mexico, switching over to Cabo San Lucas with new drinking and fishing buddies he met at the Park Central Athletic Club while volunteering at the reception desk. He has no trouble checking guys in at the athletic club and wonders why I would think so.

Three years later, in sobriety, he quit going to Cabo, and since then, he has been vacationing in Puerto Vallarta, Mexico, for sixteen years, almost the length of his sobriety. There, he found a group of Americans who were either expats or who, like him, also vacation there regularly. They form a small community: Linn and Sue from Santa Rosa, California; Señor Sunburn (George isn't sure of his actual name); John Henry with the pretty white hair and beard, from Cottonwood, Arizona; and Rip (Ty) Scott, a work friend. George goes for the recreational fishing and other forms of male bonding, minus the drinking. He fishes off the Los Muertos Pier and stays at a nearby hotel with full maid service. Someone's gotta do it. Spunky went only once. "Not my thing. And it brings back memories of my dad." And then there's always the "Let's not get too close" thing, which is humorous, because they are as close and caring with each other as any other happy couple.

He has an AA group in Mexico and attends a meeting almost every day while there, three weeks every summer. In the town next to Puerto Vallarta, there is a reform school. George and his AA group load up a bus once a week and go down there to take a meeting to the guys who are in the school for problems with drugs or alcohol. The school does things differently there—if the guys get in trouble by breaking a reform-school rule or something, they have to stand with their face to the wall, the length of the "sentence" depending on how serious the infraction was.

"There was a redheaded kid who had to stand at the wall repeatedly, and then he'd leave the treatment center and have to come back, and he just didn't want to stay sober or off drugs. I finally told him, 'Look, if you stay sober, one day you could be the first redheaded president of Mexico!'"

Only George would think of that.

In his endeavors to enrich himself intellectually, he didn't stop at college. His contacts while social-drinking at the American Legion all those years led him later to a position on the board of Arizona Boys State, a youth program of the Legion. Boys State accepts high school junior and senior boys to participate in a one-week summer program if they express an interest to their school counselors.* The annual event occurs in Flagstaff, Arizona, at Northern Arizona University. George is a senior counselor who oversees college students as they teach seminars in law and history. He oversees the students as they stay in the dorm and attend their seminars. The irony! He participates in everything they do, listening and learning. Everything except the reading and the writing. George goes every year.

"George, that's some 'high cotton,'" I said. "How do you do at it?"

"I think I'm really good at it," he said quietly. He probably is. Here's a note from a boy who experienced Boys State in 2017 with George.

Dear George,
You are by far one of the coolest, most inspirational men I have ever met in my whole life. When you said we would be family, I just thought you were some crazy old dude shooting nonsense. But I now see we actually are a family. And it is by far my favorite family. Thanks for everything. George, you really are an inspiration to us all.

Love, Jacob

I asked one day, "George, do the men who work with you at Boys State know you can't read?"

"No."

"They will after this book comes out."

He squirmed a bit. "Look, I told you at the beginning, what matters is if my story can help just one person, it'll be worth it."

What a remarkable turn of events. George, the illiterate (as he calls himself—I do not) is helping to shape the lives of adolescents who will eventually help shape their communities, and he is doing so without divulging his inability to read or write.

His friend and fellow board member Dr. Chuck Vawter concurs with George's assessment of his Boys State work. "George is great at this. He homes in on the wallflowers, the boys who stand back and aren't participating with the other guys at first. That can change a boy's life. I admire that. He's very effective."

"Dr. Vawter, what do you know about George, outside of the American Legion and his work at the phone company and such?"

"We're friends; we've known each other for several decades from the American Legion. He's a great guy."

"Do you know that he can't read or write?" George had given me permission to divulge this.

Silence. More silence.

"Dr. Vawter?"

"I did not know that."

"Now you do. He can't read at a first-grade level. Will it change his status as a member of the Boys State board? Or as a Boys State Senior Counselor?"

"Not at all."

Can I come over and pick you up off the floor, Dr. Vawter? Here you have a guy working in the renowned Boys State organization, supervising college-educated junior counselors, sitting in with the boys on all their workshops and seminars—and no one knows he can't read or write. This guy will try anything. He must have the strongest sense of survival since the caveman.

Today, at eighty-three years of age, in spite of his profound learning disability and in part because of his ongoing recovery from alcoholism, George remains physically and mentally fit. He still plays golf once a week in a foursome.

"George, do the guys in your golf foursome know you can't read?"

"Nope."

He volunteers at the Veterans' Administration once a week in the recreational activities department, working under the guidance of a recreational therapist, driving guys on field trips, playing games with them in their wheelchairs, and essentially providing friendship.

"Surely the VA knows you can't read."

"I don't think so."

"So the only people who know you don't read or write are your friends in AA."

"That's right."

"You must trust them."

"I do."

He has acquired a new smartphone and has input my phone number and address. He talks to Siri, but as is the case with most octogenarians, he doesn't use most of the programs on it—no

Wikipedia, no Twitter, no Facebook. He uses his desktop computer to check his stocks. A friend placed an icon on his screen so he sees it when the screen opens up.

"George, how well are you and Spunky 'not getting too close' as you share your retirement years?"

"Oh, I do my thing at the VA, and of course I go to Mexico every spring, but well, we do a lot together. We go to the symphony every Christmas, still go to concerts—we're going to see Tony Bennett next month at the Celebrity Theatre. Our son takes us to Huntington Beach for Thanksgiving, and a couple of years ago we won a little dance contest at a wedding! Doing the half time—we still have what it takes."

Spunky has had two basset hounds over the years, first Maurice and then Zachery. She is hesitant to get another one because of the emotional trauma of losing them to old age. She has Zachery's ashes on a cabinet in the front room, next to his picture. Instead of replacing her beloved dogs, she feeds one special tomcat of the hundreds of feral cats that live in the alleys of central Phoenix.

"For a while, she was feeding the damn pigeons out here in our yard!" exclaimed George. "I'd clean off the driveway, and pretty soon those guys would have that poop all over it! She got over that pretty quick. I'm gonna get her a bird for Christmas. I have it all planned."

*In the summer of 2017, there were 240 participants in Boys State. Among the graduates of Boys State across the country over the years are President Clinton, Walter Cronkite, Michael Jordan, and Bruce Babbitt—who were just "average boys interested in Boys State."

CHAPTER 40

Final Words

Spunky Speaks

"How DID I put up with him? It wasn't easy. He's very particular and doesn't like to be disturbed at all. Everything needs to be at his speed…and did I mention that not long after I married him, I realized he was spoiled? I think his mother and grandparents were so concerned about his reading that they may have coddled him a bit. Plus he's cheap! Just like his dad.

"I've lived a busy life, separate in some areas from his. I had my work, my friends, my sisters—we'd go to the shows in Laughlin and Las Vegas. Yes, I kissed Julio. That's a pleasant memory. We took our husbands that time.

"But George's drinking got to a point—I wasn't going to take it anymore. Fortunately, he had that wreck.

"And about the reading—why did I accept his proposal? I thought it over for a minute, and I knew I could help him."

That brings tears to my eyes. She has.

"Any regrets?"

"At times I have wondered what my life would have been like—and after fifty-six years, sometimes the reading out loud gets a bit old. He's not too insistent, but he likes to know what's going on. I still think he needs me. He thanks me all the time."

At home, Spunky and George share household tasks such as keeping the place spotless and making the morning coffee.

"George, do you help Spunky with the cooking?"

"No!" she answers emphatically from the kitchen. OK, message delivered and received.

George Speaks

"Look—I think if I had been normal, she would have shitcanned me a long time ago. I was hard on her about money—she'd want to buy something, and I don't like to buy something just to have it."

"Any worries, George?"

"I'm worried about my memory. I forget stuff I used to remember. It worries me."

"George. You're eighty-three years old. In this, you are normal. What else?"

"I've had a good life. But I don't think I've got everything done!"

You might not have, George—most of us don't—and yes, we start thinking about that as we age. And there's one thing you won't get accomplished in this lifetime, and that's learning to read and write. But obviously in your case, that isn't a life-shattering issue. It would have been nice, but would you have learned all your various clever survival skills if you had? Oh, your personality would have been, to use a slang phrase popular in the 1950s, "real George," which meant "cool," "outta sight," and "super," no matter whether you learned to read or not. But "getting everything done"? Don't worry. I suspect you'll do even more. You're only eighty-three.

"George, your story is almost told. What else is going on in your life?"

"Well, you aren't going to believe this, but I had an appointment today at the VA for my regular checkup, and the doc was looking me over for skin cancer. Guess what he found?" George lifted the hair at his hairline. "Come look at this!"

I looked closely at his hairline and saw it, right there at the front of his skull—a decades-old, inch-long scar with the widely spaced marks where the stitches had been, faint, slightly raised but hidden for so, so long.

"That's where the ball hit you! Why didn't you ever show me that before?"

"I didn't know it was there."

"What?"

"I never knew it was there."

Hold on. "Spunky? Did you never tell George he had an inch-long scar on his forehead?"

"I never saw it."

"What?" I looked closely at the scar. It's probable that his hairline receded in his old age, exposing the seventy-eight-year-old mark as his own eyes were dimming and Spunky was not gazing into his eyes as much or as often. His thick, sandy hair had obscured that evidence ever since he was a child, at school and evermore until now. It didn't show, so no one bothered to say anything to his teachers, or they never thought anything of it if they did see it.

"George, we might have discovered the cause of your illiteracy," I commented nonchalantly. Science has determined that a head injury may cause trouble with the reading process. But all these years—to not see that scar. It's as if he didn't want to see it. He didn't need to see it to give him an excuse for not reading or writing, because knowing it was there wouldn't have changed anything. He's a "no excuses" kind of guy. He carries on, as if he lived in England during the war.* He doesn't feel sorry for himself, and because nearly no one knows his secret, no one else can! Perhaps that is why he doesn't disclose it. He wants no sympathy; he wants no excuses.

George's story is not finished. To have lived such a full and rich life is the testimony of a survivor, one who faced and triumphed over major challenges. Those of us who have known him in the past and know him now are encouraged by his tenacious determination to continue overcoming not only alcoholism but a literary muteness. I only wish he could read his own story. I think he would marvel at the main character.

* Winston Churchill, the prime minister of England, told his countrymen to "carry on" when conditions were rough during World War II.

(George and Spunky in retirement)

Appendix/Notes

Reading Test Administered to George

A partial reading section of the Woodcock-Johnson mini battery was administered to George on Thursday, April 6, 2017, by Lindsay F. I listened in and observed George try to answer some of the test items.

I observed a man who knows the alphabet in order and can read the individual letters. He was asked to read some simple two-, three-, and four-letter words in a list and was able to read two of them correctly (is and get) and read several of them almost correctly, based on the first letter and other similarities—he read "can't" for *can*, "now" and then "nit" for *not*, "say" for *said*, "sin" for *since*, and "when" for *whose*. He also read "wait" for *whose*, "owned" for *once*, and "word" for *whole*. (The actual word prompts are in italics.) The fact that he misread the words that started with the blend "wh" suggests that he didn't learn to read past initial letters.

She then asked him to read some simple sentences and fill in the blank with a word that makes sense.

On the first sentence, he slowly worked out, "Your room is a _____." Using the word "room" as his key word and the picture of a boy, the word for the blank was "mess." That was correct.

The second sentence was "Ducks like to _____ in the pond." There was no picture for this sentence. He could not read *ducks*. I gave him a personal clue (Nathan, his duck). He eventually came around to "swim," but it wasn't easy.

The third sentence was "A bird has two _____." He didn't get it, reading it "as two" instead of "has two."

Stop Section I.

Next, she asked him to name the letter that makes the sound.

P. He knew it.

K. He first said *N* and then corrected it.

Stop Section II.

She showed him nonsense words, and he was to read them by sounding them out (this is a phonics test).

Word was	He read
Tiff	Tife
Zoop	Soap
Nan	Nan (Correct! That is the first syllable in my name, and he may have seen it on a phone message.)
Rax	Erox
Luhi	Lice
Epe	—

Basically, George uses contextual clues to read the simple sentences based on the few words and letters he knows to determine a word, but that works only for very simple sentences and is inefficient (he needs several attempts and isn't always correct). He reads at grade level K or 1, at the highest. He apparently was taught using a phonics method and likely whole words as well, because he does know some sounds and mistakes some whole words for others. For all intents and purposes, George is a nearly total nonreader, meaning he is alexic.

The test administrator dictated five words for him to spell (write).

Word	He wrote
In	In
He	Hed
Green	Grre
Are	Ren
Six	Set

He has a very basic memory of the letters for some sounds but not all. A child in the middle of grade one can spell more accurately than this.

References

Medical Definition of Alexia

Alexia: Loss of the ability to read or understand the written word, due either to brain damage that disconnects these functions or to temporary dysfunction caused by abnormal electrical or chemical activity in the brain.

Source:
http://www.medicinenet.com/script/main/art.asp?articlekey=6584

ALEXIA

Noun, pathology.

- A neurologic disorder marked by loss of the ability to understand written or printed language, usually resulting from a brain lesion or a congenital defect. (Dictionary.com)
- Loss of the ability to read, usually caused by brain lesions. (Gk. "A" meaning without or non; lexis meaning (in this case) reading; originally meaning speech.) (The American Heritage College Dictionary 3rd ed.)

What Causes Lesions on the Brain?

A brain lesion describes damage or destruction to any part of the brain. It may be due to trauma or any other disease that can cause inflammation, malfunction, or destruction of brain cells or brain tissue.

Sources:
http://www.medicinenet.com/brain_lesions_lesions_on_the_brain/page2.htm
http://www.webmd.com/brain/brain-lesions-causes-symptoms-treatments#3

George was indeed hit on the head, in the location of the frontal lobe on the left side of the brain, where the reading process begins. However, most of reading (memory for letters, sounds, and blending of letters and sounds to form words) occurs in the temporal lobe.

Nineteen percent of brain injuries are caused by an object striking the head. A child's skull is one-eighth the thickness of an adult's skull, thereby optimizing the chance for injury if struck. An object that strikes the head may hit at one site, but if the strike is hard enough, the brain may (and likely will) shift and bang the brain against the skull at another site, such as the site of reading acquisition, causing damage.

Sources:

https://www.medicinenet.com/brain_lesions_lesions_on_the_brain/article.htm#brain_anatomy

http://www.braininjury.com/anatomy.shtml

http://www.braininjury.com/children.shtml

Arizona Boys State

American Legion Boys State is among the most respected and selective educational programs of government instruction for US high school students. A participatory program in which students become part of the operation of local, county and state government, Boys State was founded in 1935 to counter the socialism-inspired Young Pioneer Camps. The program was the idea of two Illinois Legionnaires, Hayes Kennedy and Harold Card, who organized the first Boys State at the Illinois State Fairgrounds in Springfield. American Legion Auxiliary sponsors a separate but similar program for young women called Girls State.

At Boys State, participants learn the rights, privileges, and responsibilities of franchised citizens. The training is objective and centers on the structure of city, county, and state governments.

Operated by students elected to various offices, Boys State activities include legislative sessions, court proceedings, law-enforcement presentations, assemblies, bands, choruses, and recreational programs. Legion posts select high-school juniors to attend the program. In most cases, individual expenses are paid by a sponsoring post, a local business, or another community-based organization. Boys State programs currently exist in all Legion departments except Hawaii. As separate corporations, Boys State programs vary in content and method of procedure, but each adheres to the same basic concept: teaching government from the township to the state level.

http://arizonaboysstate.net/

Illiteracy Statistics

The US Census records report that 14 percent of US adults cannot read above a basic level. (Basic level translates into approximately third-grade reading.) If you cannot read at this level, that makes your reading ability lower than students who read in a third-grade class. That is where George is, and in fact, he is in the most disabled group of readers, people who cannot read even a primary-grade reader (grades K–2). People in this category and are living in the United States are most likely physiologically unable to learn to read. Attempting to learn at this level, after years of opportunities in school, is extremely frustrating. People who cannot read at this level are determined to have a condition called alexia, meaning the absence of reading (and not just the outdated understanding that dyslexia means only the reversal of letters.) Most poor readers, such as children who benefit from special-education remedial classes for reading, are dyslexic, which means that they have difficulty learning to read for a variety of reasons. These children can learn, and often quite well, if instructed properly after a correct diagnosis. George cannot. The condition of alexia is rare.

Source:

http://www.statisticbrain.com/number-of-american-adults-who-cant-read/

Made in the USA
Middletown, DE
13 July 2019